CONVERSATIONAL
JAPANESE

CONVERSATIONAL
JAPANESE

The Right Word at the Right Time

Anne Kaneko

TUTTLE Publishing

Tokyo | Rutland, Vermont | Singapore

Published by Tuttle Publishing, an imprint of Periplus Editions (HK) Ltd.

www.tuttlepublishing.com

Copyright © 2011 by Periplus Editions (HK) Ltd.

Library of Congress Cataloging-in-Publication Data

Kaneko, Anne.
  Conversational Japanese : the right word at the right time / Anne Kaneko. -- 1st ed.
    p. cm. In English and Japanese.
  Includes bibliographical references.
  ISBN 978-4-8053-1124-0 (pbk.)
1. Japanese language--Conversation and phrase books--English. 2. Japanese
language--Textbooks for foreign speakers--English. 3. Japanese language--Spoken
Japanese. I. Title.
  PL539.K27 2011
  495.6'83421--dc22

                    2011002817

ISBN 978-4-8053-1124-0

Distributed by

North America, Latin America & Europe
Tuttle Publishing
364 Innovation Drive
North Clarendon,
VT 05759-9436 U.S.A.
Tel: 1 (802) 773-8930
Fax: 1 (802) 773-6993
info@tuttlepublishing.com
www.tuttlepublishing.com

Japan
Tuttle Publishing
Yaekari Building, 3rd Floor
5-4-12 Osaki, Shinagawa-ku
Tokyo 141 0032
Tel: (81) 3 5437-0171
Fax: (81) 3 5437-0755
sales@tuttle.co.jp
www.tuttle.co.jp

Asia Pacific
Berkeley Books Pte. Ltd.
61 Tai Seng Avenue #02-12
Singapore 534167
Tel: (65) 6280-1330
Fax: (65) 6280-6290
inquiries@periplus.com.sg
www.periplus.com

First edition
14 13 12 11   10 5 4 3 2 1   1106MP

Printed in Singapore

TUTTLE PUBLISHING® is a registered trademark of Tuttle Publishing, a division of
Periplus Editions (HK) Ltd.

Contents

Introduction

This is a book about communication. As we all know, communication is more than just language. Our body language is just as important, and we all bring a host of personal and cultural baggage to each conversation we have. To communicate successfully in another culture we need more than the bare bones of the language. We need to understand the given norms of that society, how people interact, how things work, what the system is, how to navigate and manipulate those systems--in short, how to use the language in context.

This book aims to prepare you for situations you are likely to find yourself in if you go to Japan to visit or to work. I've worked on the assumption that if you know in advance what is likely to crop up you'll be better able to function successfully than if you come cold to a situation. Every chapter starts with a short introduction giving background knowledge for that topic; then there are dialogues based on real-life situations which give you the words and phrases you need to manage a wide range of daily tasks from getting on with the neighbors, to buying a phone, shopping on the internet, sightseeing, visiting clients or giving a speech. Many of the tasks we have to perform, such as dealing with immigration, filing a tax return or even filling up with gasoline require specialist vocabulary, and I've included that too.

This is not a programmed language course; rather, it is aimed at people who have taken such a course or have otherwise mastered the basics of the language, though I hope that even beginners picking up this book will gain confidence and proficiency in interacting with the Japanese in many ordinary situations. I hope this book fills a gap, is interesting and fun to read, and serves as a stimulus to further study.

I've tried to keep the language simple and clear and strike a balance between textbook Japanese and the colloquial language. Real life conversations are untidy and elliptical. You'll find people use far more contractions than I have done, omit particles, and add extra particles and nouns to the end of sentences. I've done this to a certain extent but in real life there will be much more.

One of the difficulties in spoken Japanese is the wide range of language, from informal to very formal. The examples in this book are standard Japanese (although in most cases the sentences are softened with informal endings). The language does veer on the polite side but you can always tone it down after observing how other people speak. It's better to start this way than be too familiar at the outset. And there are bound to be occasions when you need to summon all your linguistic talents to make a good impression. Even Japanese new recruits are put through their paces on their first day at the office, learning how to bow properly, answer the phone and use respect language correctly!

Unlike most language books, *Conversational Japanese* does not restrict the use of **kanji** (Chinese characters), and the sentences are written in the usual Japanese combination of **kana** and **kanji**. I realize that learning **kanji** is a mammoth task but I hope that by using the **romaji** that is included for each word or phrase, you will find that you can read more than you think, that as you go along the **kanji** become easier to read and easier to remember, and that you can pick up new **kanji** over time. Perhaps you already know a word but not the character: seeing the **kanji** might give you a new insight into the meaning. This can be a eureka moment, and is the fascination of the language.

I am very grateful to the publishers, Tuttle Publishing, for giving me this opportunity to pass on my knowledge to a new generation. I hope this book will, in a small way, help people get more out of their stay in Japan, help them understand Japan better and communicate more meaningfully.

The dialogues in this book are presented by a diverse group of characters. We have Lin Wenbao, a postgraduate student from Shanghai; Max and Kate Brown, English teachers from the UK living in Sendai;

Kim Young Hee, a young woman from South Korea; and Michael and Emily Taylor, from the United States. There are also Japanese characters with whom they work and interact.

I am indebted to all those past and present whom I have known over the years and who directly and indirectly contributed to my knowledge of the language and the book. All the mistakes, omissions etc. are obviously my own.

Anne Kaneko
Koriyama, Japan
October 2010

A note on pronunciation

Japanese learn good enunciation by repeating the syllabary below. The syllables should be pronounced short and crisp, staccato-like. Don't lengthen the syllables in any way or add intonation. Keep them flat. The nearest approximations in English to the five Japanese vowels are: *a* as in "ah", *i* as in "bit", *u* as in "boot", *e* as it "bet" and *o* as in bold.

a	i	u	e	o
ka	ki	ku	ke	ko
sa	shi	su	se	so
ta	chi	tsu	te	to
na	ni	nu	ne	no
ha	hi	fu	he	ho
ma	mi	mu	me	mo
ya		yu		yo
ra	ri	ru	re	ro
wa				o
n				

Most importantly, be sure to pronounce the long vowels, marked with a macron in the text (except for *ii*), by prolonging the vowel sound, again without adding intonation. If you don't make them long, it will affect the meaning and people won't understand what you're saying.

The romanized script in this book is a good guide to pronunciation but always pronounce "g" hard, as in "get." Also, the final "u" is silent in the syllable -**su**, so that **desu** is pronounced "dess." When pronouncing double consonants such as **chotto** or **zannen**, pause slightly before the second syllable.

Chapter 1 The Fundamentals

The Fundamentals

Greetings and other set expressions help any society run smoothly. In Japan, these phrases delineate relationships, offer face-saving ways to deal with difficult situations, and provide a convenient shorthand for expressing thanks or regret. In Japanese there is no need to be original; in most situations, there is no phrase better than the set phrase.

I've run through the main greetings, but you will need to follow these up with a word of thanks. When meeting in person or on the phone, people seem to have this remarkable facility for remembering your last encounter. It's embedded in the language. So use some of the follow-up expressions listed as a kind of shorthand. Just a phrase, and a set phrase at that, recreates the circumstances of the last time you met. There's no need to go into detail. With that one set phrase you have reinforced the relationship.

Relations are quite formal in Japan, with proper introductions being the norm. Again there are set phrases. After you get used to it you may find this way of dealing with people quietly reassuring.

Bowing is infectious, and after a while you'll probably start doing it too. If you're going to do it, you might as well do it right. A proper bow (**o-jigi**) is from the waist: about 15 degrees is fine for most situations. Men keep the arms straight at the sides, women place their hands in front. A nod of the head (**eshaku**) is also used for brief thanks or to acknowledge people when you meet them. No need to be obsequious, and don't stick your head out like a chicken.

This chapter also includes some notes on respect language. All languages have different levels of politeness. I've tried to explain the basic principles and there will be examples throughout the book. It's part and parcel of the language.

Finally, avoid the use of pronouns. **Anata** translates as "you" but its use is generally avoided. (One exception is when wives call their husbands **anata**—it has the special meaning of "darling.") When talking to someone, you can be safe and say his or her name, with the suffix -**san**, every time you want to say "you." Otherwise, refer to teachers, doctors, speakers, and government officials as **sensei** (teacher), and higher ranking members in your company by their titles. For example, if you want to ask your manager's opinion, say, with a rising intonation, **Kachō no o-kangae wa?** Similarly, the use of the first person pronoun meaning "I" (**watashi wa**) sounds as if you're drawing attention to yourself. Generally, it's not necessary for the sense of the sentence.

So, to get started, here are some basic greetings and phrases to use in different situations with, for your interest, some notes on their usage.

Greeting People aisatsu 挨拶

Ohayō gozaimasu お早うございます *Good Morning*

"It's early" is the literal meaning and it was originally used to thank people coming into work. It's still used in this sense in the entertainment industry when someone starting work in the afternoon will be greeted like this. Friends drop the **gozaimasu**.

Konnichi wa こんにちは *Good afternoon* or *Hello*

Used from late morning to late afternoon but not as much as Hello or **Ohayō gozaimasu**. It's not usually said to colleagues or family members. When you feel you should be polite, say **Shitsurei shimasu** (below) instead.

Konban wa こんばんは *Good Evening*

This too is somewhat more limited in its use. If you're living with a Japanese family, it might make you sound standoffish, as if you don't want to be treated like a member of the family.

Shitsurei shimasu/O-jama shimasu
失礼します / お邪魔します
Excuse me (lit. *I am about to disturb you*)

Either of these two polite expressions would be appropriate when entering or leaving someone's home or office.

Tadaima ただいま *I'm home!*

The response by those in the house is **Okaeri-nasai** お帰りなさい. Said by a waiter in a restaurant, **tadaima** means "right away".

Follow-up Expressions

Quickly think back to the last time you met the person and use one of these phrases. If you met them recently you could simply say:

- **Konaida wa dōmo.**
  こないだはどうも。
  Thank you for the other day.

Or more politely

- **Senjitsu wa dōmo arigatō gozaimashita.**
  先日はどうもありがとうございました。
  Thank you very much for the other day.

If you went to their house or they treated you to a meal, be sure to say,

- **Konaida wa dōmo gochisō-sama deshita.**
  こないだはどうもごちそうさまでした。
  Thank you for the meal/drinks the other day.

The standard reply to either of the above phrases is:

- **Kochira koso, arigato gozaimashita.**
  こちらこそ、ありがとうございました。
  On the contrary, let me thank you.

If you haven't seen the person for a while you would say:

- **Shibaraku.**   しばらく。   *It's been a long time.*

Or more politely,

- **O-hisashiburi desu / Shibaraku-buri desu ne.**
  お久しぶりです / しばらくぶりですね。
  It's been a long time.

A common response would be:

- **Go-busata shite imasu.**
  ご無沙汰しています。
  Sorry not to have been in touch.

If you meet someone important to you—for example, if you meet your child's teacher or you meet a client, your follow-up words would be:

- **Itsumo o-sewa ni natte imasu.**
  いつもお世話になっています。
  I am continually in your favor.

Or you could follow up the greeting with an enquiry into their health or their business.

- **Genki? / O-genki desu ka? / O-kawari nai desu ka?**
  元気？ / お元気ですか？ / お変わりないですか？
  You well? / Are you well? / No change? (in your health)

- **O-isogashii desu ka? / Keiki wa dō desu ka?**
  お忙しいですか？ / 景気はどうですか？
  Are you busy? / How's business?

You would respond with one of these:

- **Mā-mā desu ne. / Hai, o-kagesama de.**
  まあまあですね。 / はい、おかげさまで。
  Not bad. / Fine, thank you (lit. *thanks to you*).

Osaka businessmen greet each other with **Mōkarimakka?** 儲かりまっか？ (*lit.* Making money?). The standard reply is **bochi-bochi** ぼちぼち or **botsu-botsu** ぼつぼつ both meaning "a bit at a time".

Dōmo/Dōmo dōmo どうも / どうもどうも *Thanks*

This is an all-encompassing expression of thanks and apology widely used, especially by men. It can be combined with almost any of the other set expressions in this chapter, e.g. **Dōmo, konnichi wa** どうもこんにちは and **Dōmo, o-hisashiburi** どうも、お久しぶり.

Commenting on the Weather
kisetsu no aisatsu 季節の挨拶

To get the conversation going, you can always say something about the weather. Here's a selection that should get you through most days.

- **Samui desu ne** 寒いですね。 *It's cold, isn't it?*

- **Futte kimashita ne** 降ってきましたね。
  It's started to rain, hasn't it?

- **Haremashita ne** 晴れましたね。
  It's cleared up, hasn't it?

- **Uttōshii tenki desu ne** うっとうしい天気ですね。
  It's dreary weather, isn't it?

- **Atatakaku narimashita ne** 暖かくなりましたね。
  It's really warming up, isn't it?

- **Ii o-tenki desu ne** 良いお天気ですね。
  It's beautiful weather, isn't it?

- **Atsukute, taihen desu ne** 暑くてたいへんですね。
  It's awfully hot, isn't it?

- **Mushi-atsui desu ne** 蒸し暑いですね。
  It's hot and humid, isn't it?

- **Ijō kishō desu ne** 異常気象ですね。
  This is abnormal weather, isn't it?

Being Introduced
shōkai 紹介

When meeting someone for the first time, most people use the following set expression:

- **Hajimemashite. Dōzo yoroshiku o-negai shimasu.**
  はじめまして。どうぞよろしくお願いします。
  How do you do? Pleased to meet you.

This expression points out that it is a first-time meeting and then asks for the other person's favorable consideration. The standard reply is:

- **Kochira koso. Dōzo yoroshiku.**
  こちらこそ。どうぞよろしく。
  The pleasure's mine. Glad to meet you.

Saying Goodbye
wakareru 別れる

Sayōnara さようなら　*Goodbye* (lit. *If it must be so*)

Unfortunately, this famous and romantic farewell is not used so much. Although schoolchildren are taught to say **Sayōnara** to their teachers at the end of the school day, adults don't usually use it in ordinary situations. **Sayōnara** is mostly used between friends when they are parting for a long time; for example, when they are seeing someone off who is moving away.

Shitsurei shimashita　失礼しました
Goodbye (lit. *I have imposed*)

This polite phrase is used in business situations, at social gatherings, or when leaving someone's home.

Mata ne!　またね　**Ja ne!**　じゃね　*See you! Bye!*

This is how friends say goodbye. Variations include **Mata ashita** また明日 See you tomorrow; **Mata raishū** また来週 See you next week; and じゃーまた **Ja mata**.

Baibai　バイバイ　*Bye-bye*

Used by young people, especially children.

Gochisō-sama deshita　ごちそうさまでした
Thank you. It was delicious

You say this as soon as you've finished eating but it's often repeated when saying goodbye to someone who has treated you to a meal (or even to just a cup of tea). You can also say it to restaurant staff when leaving the premises.

O-yasumi-nasai おやすみなさい *Good night*

Frequently used also on the phone, this is how friends and family say good night. It's not used, however, when you leave work; it would imply that those remaining at the office would sleep there until morning! Use **O-saki ni** instead.

O-saki ni お先に
Goodbye (lit. *Excuse me for going ahead of you*)

This expression (the more polite form is **O-saki ni shitsurei shimasu** お先に失礼します) is used when leaving a group of friends or colleagues. The appropriate response in work situations would be **O-tsukare-sama deshita** お疲れ様でした Goodbye. Thank you for your help.

Itte kimasu 行ってきます
Goodbye. I'm off! (lit. *I'll go and come back*)

This phrase, whose more polite form is **Itte mairimasu** 行ってまいります, is used when leaving home. It's also used during working hours when people temporarily leave their offices. The appropriate response by those remaining would be **Itte' rasshai** 行ってらっしゃい, (*lit.* Go and come back).

O-daiji ni お大事に *Take care of your health*

This friendly phrase is used when taking leave of the elderly or of someone who is sick or injured.

Go-kigen yō ごきげんよう *Farewell*

This can sound either refined or affected depending on the circumstances. Although people rarely say this, it's occasionally still heard at the end of television shows.

Ja, ki o tsukete　じゃ、気をつけて　*Take care*

This casual farewell phrase is used between friends. More polite, but still friendly, equivalents are **O-ki o tsukete** お気をつけて and **O-genki de** お元気で.

Expressing Gratitude
kansha　感謝

There are several ways to say "thank you", from informal to very polite. They are:

Arigatō　ありがとう
Dōmo arigatō　どうもありがとう
Arigatō gozaimasu　ありがとうございます, and
Dōmo arigatō gozaimasu　どうもありがとうございます.

You can also use the past tense **gozaimashita**. As a general rule, when the action is happening or will happen, say **Arigatō gozaimasu**, for example, when you are being handed a present. When the action is completed, say **Arigatō gozaimashita**, for example, when you have received a present in the mail and are thanking the sender by phone. An appropriate response is **Dō itashimashite** どういたしまして You're welcome, or **Kochira koso** こちらこそ On the contrary, let me thank you.

Sumimasen　すみません　*Thank you*

This is an apology but is often used to thank someone when you've put them to some trouble. Similar expressions include: **O-tesū o kakemashita** お手数を掛けました and ご迷惑をかけました **Go-meiwaku o kakemashita**. In response, say **Dō itashimashite** どういたしまして You're welcome, or **O-kamai naku** おかまいなく No worries.

O-sewa ni narimashita 　お世話になりました
I'm obliged to you

This is the best way to thank someone who has spent time helping you. When you want to thank someone who has shown you around, say something like:

- **O-sewa ni narimashita. Go-annai itadaite, yokatta desu.**
  お世話になりました。ご案内いただいて、よかったです。
  Thank you very much for all your kindness. It was great having you take us around.

Tasukarimashita 　助かりました 　*You've been a great help*

If someone has helped you with a translation, you can thank them like this:

- **O-kage-sama de shimekiri ni ma-ni-atte, tasukarimashita.**
  おかげさまで締め切りに間に合って、助かりました。
  Thanks to you I made the deadline. You were a great help.

Go-kurō-sama 　ご苦労様 　*Thank you for your help*

This is a traditional phrase expressing appreciation to someone who has finished working. You can use it to thank someone who's done a job or service for you. It may be inappropriate when addressing superiors and you might be better off using **O-tsukare-sama** instead.

O-tsukare-sama 　お疲れ様 　*Thank you for your help/work*

Originating in the entertainment world this is now interchangeable with **Go-kurō-sama**, and perhaps more widely used. When a colleague leaves the office to go home and says **O-saki ni** お先に, respond with **O-tsukare-sama**.

Kyōshuku desu　恐縮です　　**Osoreiremasu**　恐れ入れます
I am very grateful

The literal meaning of these phrases is "I shrink with fear (in the face of your great kindness)". If someone has unexpectedly done something nice to you, you can offer thanks by saying:

- **Sorewa sorewa, dōmo, kyōshuku desu.**
  それはそれはどうも。恐縮です。
  This really is too much. Thank you.

Itadakimasu　いただきます　　*Thank you* (lit. *I receive*)

Everyone says this before starting a meal or snack. **Itadakimasu** is the humble form of the verb **morau**, to receive, and is used extensively in respect language.

Gochisō-sama deshita　ごちそうさまでした
Thank you (lit. *It was a feast*)

This is how you say "thank you" when finishing a meal or snack.

1.07　A Few Notes on Respect Language　keigo　敬語

Although respect language is a vestige of feudal hierarchy, its function today is not to emphasize differences in status but more to facilitate relationships. It is used most often in business, on formal occasions, and when meeting people for the first time.

For the vast majority of everyday situations, the –**masu** form of the verb which shows respect to the person you are talking to, is sufficiently polite. So, if you want to ask your girlfriend what time she's going out, you might say **Itsu dekakeru no?** いつ出かけるの？ but to ask her father when he is going out, you would say **Itsu dekakemasu ka?** いつ出かけますか

Polite forms of words, such as **ikaga** instead of **dō**, meaning "how", and **dochira** instead of **dare** meaning "who" make speech sound more refined. You'll find that speech is quite formal in business situations and these polite words are often used to add gravitas to the speech (see the chapter on Business).

The heart of respect language, however, lies in the verbs. They work on a see-saw principle. Humble verbs, referring to yourself, lower your position vis-à-vis the other person whereas honorific verbs referring to others, raise their status relative to yours. We've already met **o-negai shimasu** which is the humble form of **negaimasu** (to request). Most regular verbs follow certain rules but, as in most languages, the most common verbs are exceptions. Fortunately there are only a handful of these to learn. The verb "to go" **iku**, for example, has the humble form **mairu** and the honorific form **irassharu**. So you might say:

- **Kore kara mihonichi e mairimasu ga, go-issho ni irasshaimasen ka?**
  これから見本市へ参りますが、ご一緒にいらっしゃいませんか。
  *We (humble, **mairu**) are going on to the trade fair. Won't you (honorific **irassharu**) go with us?*

Take a look at the list at the end of the book for the special forms of these verbs and for an explanation of the use of the passive tense which is also used to show respect and which you will hear frequently.

It gets a bit tricky when you're talking about someone else. For example, when a member of staff wants to say to a colleague that the boss is out, they might say **Shacho wa irasshaimasen** (社長はいらっしゃいません), using the honorific form **irassharu** about the boss. But when speaking to a visitor they would say, **Shacho wa orimasen** (社長

はおりません), using the humble form **oru**. Within the company, the president is referred to with respectful speech, but outside the company, with humble speech. When talking to outsiders, use respectful speech about them, their boss, and their children, and humble speech about yourself, your boss and your organization.

1.08 Apologizing ayamaru 謝る

A first reaction in many situations is to apologize. All apologies should be accompanied by bows, or at least a nod of the head.

Sumimasen すみません *I'm sorry.*

Besides being the most widely used apology, this is also used to attract attention and to express thanks. The polite form is **Dōmo sumimasen deshita** どうもすみませんでした.

Shitsurei shimashita 失礼しました *I'm sorry*

This is recommended for business situations. If you accidentally interrupt your boss when he has a visitor, you can say:

- **A, shitsurei shimashita. Mata kimasu.**
  ア、失礼しました。また来ます。
  Oh, I'm sorry. I'll come back later.

Mōshiwake arimasen 申し訳ありません
I'm very sorry (lit. *There is no excuse*)

This is even more polite.

O-matase shimashita　お待たせしました
Sorry to have kept you waiting

A courteous way to apologize to someone who has been kept waiting. Used frequently on the phone.

Gomen-nasai　ごめんなさい　*Sorry*

Repentant children bow their heads and say this when they've done wrong. Since by itself it can sound too familiar, you might want to follow it with more apologies. For example:

- **Gomen-nasai. Sumimasen deshita. Daijōbu desu ka?**
  ごめんなさい。すみませんでした。大丈夫ですか。
  Oh, pardon. I'm sorry. Are you all right?

Asking Permission
yurushi o eru　許しを得る

A simple way to ask permission is to use the **-te** (or **-de**) form of a verb and attach **ii desu ka**? Adding **mo** after the verb adds emphasis to the request.

- **Haitte (mo) ii desu ka?**
  入って(も)いいですか。
  May I come in?

If a situation requires tact, you might want to use a rather complicated construction the literal meaning of which is: "May I receive from you …", using the verb **morau** (もらう) to receive. For example:

- **Ashita yasumasete moraemasu ka?**
  あした休ませてもらえますか。
  Could I please have tomorrow off? (lit. *Could I receive you having caused me to take time off?*)

You can make this more polite by using **itadaku** (いただく) instead of **morau** (もらう). And when you need to choose your words very carefully, instead of asking directly, you can say you would like to receive but …

- **Ashita yasumasete itadakitai no desu ga.**
  あした休ませていただきたいのですが。
  Could you possibly let me have tomorrow off?

This is humble because of the causative **yasumasete**, polite because of the humble **itadakitai**, and softened because of the **desu ga …** No one will be able to withhold their permission in the face of such politeness!

Making Requests
o-negai　お願い

This is the most common and widely used expression. You will hear it all the time.

- **Yoroshiku o-negai shimasu/itashimasu.**
  よろしくお願いします ／ いたします。
  Please. (lit. *I request.*)

When asking for someone on the phone, say, for example:

- **Yamada-san, o-negai shimasu.**
  山田さん、お願いします。
  Mr Yamada, please.

Kudasai　下さい　*Please*

Generally speaking, this is used in two ways. When it follows a noun, **kudasai** means "give (me)".

- **Kyo no ranchi kudasai.**
  今日のランチ, 下さい。
  May I have today's lunch?

When used after the **-te** form of a verb, **kudasai** means "Please".

- **Ashita kite kudasai.**
  あした来てください。
  Please come tomorrow.

If you wish to be more polite, replace **kudasai** with **kudasaimasen ka**?

- **Nihongo o oshiete kudasaimasen ka?**
  日本語を教えてくださいませんか。
  Would you please teach me Japanese?

The two verbs meaning to receive, **morau** (もらう) and the politer **itadaku** (いただく), are widely used when making requests. Negative forms of these verbs make the request more polite.

- **Chotto matte itadakemasu ka?**
  ちょっと待っていただけますか。
  Would you mind waiting a moment?

- **Sumimasen. Kore o dokete moraemasen ka.**
  すみません。これをどけてもらえませんか。
  Excuse me. Would you mind moving this?

1.11　Leading up to a Request

Rather than abruptly making a request, you might prepare the listener for what is to follow by starting with one of these phrases.

- **Ashita no kaigi no koto nan desu ga,**
  明日の会議のことなんですが、
  About tomorrow's meeting,

- **Jitsu wa, o-negai ga atte, o-denwa shita wake nan' desu ga,**
  実は、お願いがあって、お電話したわけなんですが、
  I phoned because there was something I wanted to ask you,

- **O-isogashii tokoro, sumimasen.**
  お忙しいところすみません。
  I'm sorry to disturb you when you're busy.

1.12

Refusing Requests
kotowaru 断る

Although refusals should be made discreetly, it is important to make it clear whether you are refusing or accepting. At the first hint of something undesirable, you might want to make a remark such as:

- **So desu ne …** そうですね。 *Well …*

When the request comes, it is often enough to say:

- **Sā, chottto …** さー、ちょっと、 *Well, it's just that …*

When spoken hesitantly, with pauses before and after the **chotto**, either of the phrases below should convey your desire not to partake.

- **Konogoro, chotto, shigoto ga isogashikute,**
  このごろ、ちょっと、仕事が忙しくて、
  I'm rather busy at work these days.

- **Saikin, chotto, taichō o kuzushimashite,**
  最近、ちょっと、体調を崩しまして、
  I've really not been feeling well recently.

If you cannot think of a specific reason, you could play for time:

- **Chotto sōdan shite, mata o-denwa shimasu.**
  ちょっと相談して、またお電話します。
  I'll discuss it (with someone) and call you back.

- **Chotto kangaesasete kudasai. Daiji na koto desu kara.**
  ちょっと考えさせてください。大事なことですから。
  Please let me think it over. It's such an important matter.

Obviously, specific excuses make convincing refusals:

- **Sumimasen ga, kyūyō ga dekimashita no de.**
  すみませんが、急用ができましたので。
  I'm sorry, but something urgent has come up.

- **Zannen desu ga, hatsuka wa tsugō ga warui no desu ga.**
  残念ですが、二十日は都合が悪いのですが。
  I'm afraid I'm not free on the twentieth.

- **Hidoi kaze o hiite shimatte, utsuru to ikenai desu kara.**
  ひどい風邪を引いてしまって、うつるといけないですから。
  I've got a terrible cold. I wouldn't like you to get it.

In cases when your reasons still do not convince the listener, you can try one of these statements:

- **Mōshi-wake arimasen ga, konkai wa o-yaku ni tatemasen no de.**
  申し訳ありませんが、今回はお役に立てませんので。
  I'm sorry but I can't help you this time.

- **Zannen desu ga, kondo wa enryo sasete itadakimasu.**
  残念ですが、今度は遠慮させていただきます。
  I'm sorry but I'll forgo it this time.

- **Demo komarimasu.**
  でも困ります。
  But that would put me in a bind.

On the other side of the coin, you may fall victim to a reluctance to give a direct refusal. There is a tendency to stress the positive "I really would like to go" and not the negative "but I can't." For example, the following phrase, depending on the context, might be a well-meaning delaying tactic:

- **Maemuki ni kentō sasete itadakitai to kangaemasu.**
  前向きに検討させていただきたいと考えます。
  We will consider it constructively.

The oblique phrase and hesitant tone may well signal that the situation is difficult. One must learn to read between the lines.

Chapter 2 The Neighborhood

The Neighborhood

Traditionally, one's neighbors were the three houses across the street and the houses on each side. This close-knit unit operated like one big family with neighbors exchanging food, helping at funerals, and sharing gifts. With increased mobility and the rise in single households this neighborhood network has disintegrated, sometimes with tragic consequences, and efforts are being made by the government, local government agencies, individuals and self-help groups to find new ways for neighbors to look out for each other.

But some of the traditions live on. When you move to a new neighborhood or apartment you should introduce yourself to your immediate neighbors. At other times giving a few homemade cookies or sharing something from your country will be interpreted as a gesture of friendship. You will certainly receive something in return.

Addresses refer to blocks, not to streets: three numbers separated by a dash. The first is the local neighborhood block, the **chōme**. Within this are perhaps ten to twenty sub-blocks called **banchi**. If you look at a map, you'll see these do follow some sort of order, but if you're walking along a street the numbers are not in sequence. The last number in the address is the number of the house, again not in sequence along a street. Signs on lamp-posts indicate the name of the **chōme** and the numbers of the **chōme** and the **banchi** but Japanese addresses are notoriously difficult to find. Give good directions and send a good map if you invite someone to your home.

Living in a Japanese community entails certain responsibilities. Dues may have to be paid to the town association. Trash is to be put out only on certain days, and in some areas people take turns cleaning the collection point after the garbage truck has left. Neighbors may not look kindly on those who do not abide by these communal rules.

If you want to play an active part in your community, the town association (**chōnaikai**) will be only too happy to have your help. These bodies, linked both with the city or ward office and with the police and fire departments, are responsible primarily for disseminating information on health, sanitation and the environment. They also organize outings, local festivals and other community activities. You can join the Sunday morning weeding group or the pest-control squad, help supervise baseball practice for children, or participate in planning (and celebrating) the local festival.

You might find that your Japanese neighbors are more tolerant than you are. The prevailing attitude is one of give-and-take (**otagai-sama**). You put up with their noisy dog and they tolerate your noisy children; your guests can park in front of their gate if their guests can park in front of yours. If you will be the source of disturbance, you can smooth relations with a prior warning or, failing that, an explanation afterward.

If you are new to the area, ask your neighbors about nearby stores, schools, doctors and so forth. The police in the neighborhood police box (**kōban**) may be able to make recommendations. The Yakult lady who delivers sweet yogurt-type drinks by bicycle, the parcel delivery people, and others who pass through regularly know the entire area and are mines of information. Don't be afraid to try local markets and family-run shops. You'll be surprised how much even a little Japanese will make your day-to-day living in Japan more enjoyable.

 **Calling on the Neighbors**

Your neighbors will probably be the group of five to ten houses around which notices are circulated; if you live in an apartment, they might be the tenants on your floor and perhaps those who share the same staircase. In Japan, a new arrival visits the neighbors, often distributing small gifts.

LIN:

Gomen kudasai. Tonari ni hikkoshimashita Rin desu. Dōzo yoroshiku.

ご免ください。隣に引っ越しました林です。どうぞよろしく。

Hello. My name is Lin and I've just moved in next door. Pleased to meet you.

WOMAN:

Kochira koso. Wazawaza arigato gozaimashita. Nihon wa nagai desu ka?

こちらこそ。わざわざありがとうございました。日本は長いですか。

The pleasure's mine. Thank you. Have you been in Japan long?

LIN:

Sangatsu kara desu.

三月からです。

Since March.

WOMAN:

Nihongo wa o-jōzu desu ne. Komatta koto ga attara, osshatte kudasai ne.

日本語はお上手ですね。困ったことがあったら、おっしゃってくださいね。

Your Japanese is very good. If you're having trouble with anything, please ask.

LIN:

Arigatō gozaimasu. De wa, sassoku desu ga, gomi wa itsu daseba ii desu ka?

ありがとうございます。では、さっそくですが、ゴミはいつ出せばいいですか。

Thank you. Well, for starters I was wondering when to put the trash out.

WOMAN:

Moeru-gomi wa getsu, kin. Petto bottoru, purasuchikku no risaikuru wa kayōbi desu. Karendā o sashiagmashō. Asa hachi-ji made ni kanrinin-shitsu no ura ni daseba ii desu.

燃えるゴミは月、金。ペットボトル、プラスチックのリサイクルは火曜日です。カレンダーを差し上げましょう。朝八時までに管理人室の裏に出せばいいです。

Burnable refuse is picked up on Mondays and Fridays. PET bottles and plastics for recycling are picked up on Tuesdays. You have to put it behind the caretaker's apartment by 8:00 a.m.

LIN:

Arigatō gozaimasu. Ja, yoroshiku o-negai shimasu.

ありがとうございます。じゃ、よろしくお願しします。

Thank you. Well, I look forward to seeing you again.

2.02 Buying Sweet Potatoes

On cold winter evenings, the potato seller drives around the neighborhood tempting customers with the melodic, plaintive song **i-shi-ya-ki imo** 石焼きいも (stone-baked potatoes). Why not try one?

KIM:

Konban wa. O-negai shimasu. Ikura desu ka?

こんばんは。お願いします。いくらですか。

Good evening. Can I have one please? How much are they?

POTATO SELLER:

Sanbyaku-en to yonhyaku en.

300円と400円。

Three hundred yen and four hundred yen.

KIM:

Sanbyaku-en no mono, ikko kudasai. Sen-en shika nai desu kedo.

300円のもの、一個ください。1,000円しかないですけど。

One at three hundred yen, please. I only have a thousand yen (note).

POTATO SELLER:

Hai. O-tsuri. Dōmo.

はい。おつり。どうも。

Here's your change. Thanks.

2.03 Asking About Restaurants

In this dialogue, Max asks a neighbor to recommend a congenial watering hole.

MAX:

Konnichi wa.

こんにちは。

Hello.

NEIGHBOR:

Konnichi wa.
こんにちは。
Hello.

MAX:

Mainichi atsui desu ne.
毎日暑いですね。
It's been so hot every day, hasn't it?

NEIGHBOR:

Hontō ne.
本当ね。
It certainly has been.

MAX:

Tokoro de, konaida mukō no yakitoriya e itte mitara, oishiku mo nai shi, omomuki mo nai shi, yoku nakatta desu yo. Motto Nihon-rashii tokoro, wakarimsen ka?
ところで、こないだ、向こうの焼き鳥屋へ行ってみたら、おいしくもないし、趣もないし、よくなかったですよ。もっと日本らしいところ、分かりませんか？
By the way, the other day I went to the yakitori restaurant across the way but it wasn't good: the food wasn't good and it had no atmosphere. Do you know somewhere more typically Japanese?

NEIGHBOR:

Nihon-rashii tokoro nē. Eki no higashi-guchi atari ni mukashi kara no izakaya ga nangen arimasu kedo ne.
日本らしいところねえ。駅の東口辺りに昔からの居酒屋が何軒ありますけどね。
Typically Japanese, eh? On the east side of the station there are several bars that have been there for a long time.

MAX:

Sō desu ka. Eki no higashi-guchi. Sono uchi, itte mimasu yo. Arigatō gozaimasu.

そうですか。駅の東口。その内、行ってみますよ。ありがとうございます。

I see. The east exit of the station. I'll go and check them out some time. Thank you very much.

2.04 Ordering a Restaurant Delivery

You can order pizzas for home delivery and if you're lucky your local noodle shop may still deliver. Rinse any empty dishes and leave them outside your door. They will be picked up later.

KATE:

Demae, o-negai dekimasu ka?

出前、お願いできますか。

Do you deliver?

RESTAURANT STAFF:

Hai dōzo.

はい、どうぞ。

Yes, go ahead.

KATE:

Shōyu rāmen, mittsu o-negai ne.

しょうゆラーメン三つ、お願いね。

Three bowls of soy sauce noodles, please.

RESTAURANT STAFF:

Hai, dochira-sama deshō ka?
はい、どちら様でしょうか。
OK. Who's speaking, please?

KATE:

Pāku Manshon sanbyaku ni gōshitsu no Buraun desu. Na-rubeku hayaku o-negai shimasu.
パークマンションの三百二号室のブラウンです。なるべく早くお願いします。
Brown. Apartment 302, Park Mansion. As quick as you can please.

RESTAURANT STAFF:

Hai, tadaima.
はい、ただいま。
Fine. We'll be right over.

2.05 Admiring a Neighbor's Garden

Small, potted azaleas are a mass of flowers in May and June, and most enthusiasts will be delighted to show you their collection. (Note: the ending **ka shira** is only used by women.)

KIM:

Ii tenki desu ne. Niwa-shigoto desu ka?
いい天気ですね。庭仕事ですか。
Beautiful day, isn't it? I see you're doing some gardening.

NEIGHBOR:

Ē, chotto.
ええ、ちょっと。
Yes, a few odd jobs.

KIM:

Mā, migoto na tsutsuji desu ne! Chotto mite ii ka shira?
まあ、見事なつつじですね。ちょっと見ていいかしら？
Those really are splendid azaleas! May I take a look?

NEIGHBOR:

Dōzo, dōzo. Naka ni haitte mite kudasai.
どうぞ、どうぞ。中に入って見て下さい。
Please do. Come inside and have a look.

KIM:

Kore wa nensū ga tatte iru deshō ne.
これは年数がたっているでしょうね。
This one must be very old.

NEIGHBOR:

Hyaku-nijū-nen mae no mono desu yo.
百二十年前のものですよ。
It's 120 years old.

KIM:

Kanroku ga arimasu ne. Tenji-kai ni dasun' desu ka?
かんろくがありますね。展示会に出すんですか。
It's very impressive. Will you enter them in an exhibition?

NEIGHBOR:

Ē. Ima sono junbi ni kakatte irun' desu yo.
ええ。今その準備にかかっているんですよ。
Yes. I'm getting them ready for one right now.

KIM:

Subarashii desu. Arigatō gozaimashita.
すばらしいです。ありがとうございました。
Wonderful. Thank you very much.

NEIGHBOR:

Iie. Mata dōzo.
いいえ、またどうぞ。
Not at all. Come again.

Warning Neighbors About a Party

2.06

Your neighbors will appreciate being warned that you plan to have a party and that it may be noisy.

MAX:

Konban wa.
こんばんは。
Good evening.

NEIGHBOR:

Dōzo, dōzo.
どうぞ、どうぞ。
Do come in. (lit. Please, please.)

MAX:

Iya, genkan-saki de shitsurei shimasu. Anō, ashita no ban, to-modachi no sayōnara pātei o uchi de suru koto ni natchai-mashite, sukoshi urusai ka mo shiremasen ga yoroshiku o-negai shimasu.
いや、玄関先で失礼します。あのう、明日の晩、友達のさようならパーテイを家ですることになっちゃいまして、少しうるさいかも知れませんが、よろしくお願いします。
No, I'm fine here at the door. I've just come to tell you that I'll be giving a farewell party for a friend tomorrow evening. It may turn out to be rather noisy but I hope we don't disturb you.

NEIGHBOR:

Iie. O-tagai-sama desu kara. Waza-waza dōmo.
いいえ、お互い様ですから。わざわざどうも。
That's all right. Next time it'll probably be us. Thanks for telling us.

MAX:

Dōzo yoroshiku.
どうぞよろしく。
Thank you.

2.07 Complaining About Noise

When you have to say something tactfully try to speak hesitantly, waiting for a nod or word of agreement from the other before continuing. In this dialogue, Lin politely asks the neighbors to do something about a noisy dryer.

LIN:

Itsumo o-sewa ni natte imasu.
いつもお世話になっています。
Thank you for always being so good to me.

NEIGHBOR:

Iie.
いいえ。
Not at all.

LIN:

Jitsu wa hijō ni ii-nikui no desu ga, otaku no kansōki no oto ga gata-gata to uchi ni hibikimashite, yoku nerarenain' desu.
実は、非常に言いにくいのですが、お宅の乾燥機の音がガタガタと家に響きまして、よく寝られないんです。
I don't know how to say this, but even from my apartment, I can hear your dryer clattering so much that I haven't been able to sleep.

NEIGHBOR:

A, sō desu ka?
あ、そうですか。
Oh, I didn't realize.

LIN:

Osoku made kakimono o suru toki mo arimasu shi, yabun wa narubeku oto ga morenai yō ni o-negai dekinai deshō ka?

遅くまで書き物をする時もありますし、夜分はなるべく音が漏れないようにお願いできないでしょうか。

Sometimes I stay up late writing so I really would appreciate it if you would try not to make so much noise at night.

NEIGHBOR:

Hai, wakarimashita. Mōshi-wake arimasen deshita.

はい、分かりました。申し訳ありませんでした。

I see. I'm very sorry.

LIN:

Yoroshiku o-negai itashimasu.

よろしくお願いいたします。

Thank you very much.

2.08   Asking Someone to Move a Car

If you need to have a neighbor move a car, a quick conversation through the interphone should suffice.

MICHAEL:

Sumimasen. Tonari no Tērā desu ga, kuruma o ugokashite kudasaimasen ka?

すみません。隣のテーラーですが、車を動かしてくださいませんか。

Excuse me. This is Taylor from next door. Would you mind moving your car?

NEIGHBOR:

Sumimasen. Sugu ikimasu.
すみません。すぐ行きます。
I'm sorry. I'll be right there.

2.09 Apologizing to a Neighbor

Apologies should be spoken in a quiet voice and accompanied with bows. In this dialogue, Kate apologizes for a broken window.

KATE:

Dōmo mōshiwake arimasen. Kodomo ga mado-garasu o watte shimatte, taihen go-meiwaku o kakemashita. O-kega wa arimasen deshita ka?
どうも、申し訳ありません。子供が窓ガラスを割ってしまって、たいへんご迷惑を掛けました。お怪我はありませんでしたか。
We're terribly sorry for all the trouble our child caused when he broke your window. Was anyone hurt?

NEIGHBOR:

Kega wa arimasen deshita yo.
怪我はありませんでしたよ。
No, no one was hurt.

KATE:

Aa, sore wa yokatta. Harawasete itadakimasu no de, seikyūsho o o-mawashi kudasai. Hontō ni mōshiwake arimasen deshita.
あら、それはよかった。払わせていただきますので、請求書をお回しください。本当に申し訳ありませんでした。
Oh, I'm so glad to hear that. We'll pay (lit. We will let you make us pay) so please send the bill to us. I really do apologize.

2.10 Reporting a Robbery

A house break-in is reported to the policeman on duty at the neighborhood police box.

MICHAEL:

Sumimasen. Yūbe dorobō ni hairarete, genkin o nusumaremashita. Dō sureba ii desu ka?

すみません。夕べどろぼうに入られて、現金を盗まれました。どうすればいいですか。

Excuse me. Last night our house was broken into and some money was stolen. What should we do?

POLICEMAN:

O-namae to jūsho o oshiete kudasai.

お名前と住所を教えてください。

Tell me your name and address.

MICHAEL:

Namae wa Tērā. Jūsho wa Nakano san-chōme jū-roku-banchi no yon-gō desu.

名前はテーラー。住所は、中野三丁目十六番地の四号です。

My name is Taylor . My address is Nakano 3-16-4.

POLICEMAN:

Dewa, chotto matte kudasai. Issho ni ikimasu kara.

では、ちょっと待ってください。一緒に行きますから。

Well, just a moment. I'll go with you (to the house).

2.11 Going on Vacation

If you go on vacation, you might want to ask one of your neighbors to keep an eye on the house. Emily begins by explaining why she has come to see her neighbor.

EMILY:

Jitsu wa, o-negai ga atte mairimashita. Ashita kara Amerika e kaeru no de, ikkagetsu rusu ni suru koto ni narimashita. Shujin no kaisha no denwa bangō ga koko ni kaite okimashita no de, nanika arimashitara, go-renraku itadakemasen ka?

実は、お願いがあってまいりました。明日からアメリカへ帰るので、一ヶ月留守にすることになりました。主人の会社の電話番号がここに書いておきましたので、何かありましたら、ご連絡いただけませんか。

Actually, I want to ask you a favor. We're leaving for the United States tomorrow and the house will be vacant for a month. I've written down the telephone number of my husband's office. Would you get in touch (with the office) if anything happens?

NEIGHBOR:

Hai, wakarimashita. Ii desu ne. Yukkuri tanoshinde kite kudasai.

はい、分かりました。いいですね。ゆっくり楽しんできてください。

Yes, I certainly will. And I hope you have a nice, relaxing time.

EMILY:

Arigatō gozaimasu. Yoroshiku o-negai shimasu.

ありがとうございます。よろしくお願いします。

Thank you. And thanks for keeping an eye on the house.

2.12 Words and Expressions

kōban	交番	*police box*
chōnai-kai	町内会	*town association*
chōnai-kaichō	町内会長	*chairman of the town association*
chōnai-kaihi	町内会費	*town association dues*
kairanban	回覧板	*notice board passed around the neighborhood*
ie/uchi	家	*one's own home*
o-taku	お宅	*your home or house*
jūkyo/jūtaku	住居・住宅	*house, dwelling*
jūtaku-chi	住宅地	*residential area*
danchi	団地	*apartment complex*
ikken-ya	一軒家	*detached house*
manshon	マンション	*apartment, condominium*
apāto	アパート	*apartment (usually one with a comparatively inexpensive rent)*
kanri-nin	管理人	*caretaker*
tsubo	坪	*old Japanese unit for measuring land area and floor space; equivalent to two mats (to convert tsubo to square meters, multiply by 3.3)*
tachi-banashi o suru	立ち話をする	*stand chatting*

Chapter 3 The Telephone

The Telephone

Telephoning in any foreign language can be daunting, for without facial expressions and other clues it's harder to understand what's being said. People may speak faster than you'd like and service staff in particular may speak very polite Japanese, which can be hard to follow.

As with the language generally, there are set phrases for use on the phone, and you can start by learning and applying these. The most common, of course, is **moshi-moshi** (Hello). A wonderfully expressive phrase, **moshi-moshi** conjures up images of frustrated callers trying to get connected in the early days of the telephone. As well as using this when answering the phone, people also use it during a conversation just to make sure the other person is still there.

Many of the follow-up phrases introduced in the first chapter are used on the phone. **Konaida wa dōmo** (Thank you for the other day) is used very frequently even when there is nothing in particular that requires thanks. This and other expressions of gratitude, denial, and inquiry are usually mentioned before stating the reason for the call. Often these are spoken at breakneck speed until the caller arrives at **Jitsu wa** (Well, the reason I'm calling is. . .). If you cannot match this speed, try to hold your own with other, albeit abbreviated, phrases such as **iie**, **dōmo**, and **kochira koso**.

The language used on the phone runs the gamut from very informal to highly stylized. You might hear someone answer the phone very politely then, realizing the caller is a friend, flip into informal speech. The difference is instant and extreme and, if you're an observer, can be quite funny. In conversations where you feel you need to be polite, follow the usual rule: use the –**masu** form of the verbs. This should see you through most situations. If you want to be extra polite, you can use humble verbs about yourself. For instance, instead of saying **kiki-masu** (I ask) you can say **o-kiki shimasu**. Likewise, **o-denwa shimasu** (I'm telephoning). To ask if someone is there you can use an honorific verb about that person, **irasshaimasu ka**? There are guidelines and more examples in this chapter.

The Japanese cell phone (**keitai**) has developed its own culture and many young people seem to have phones stuck to their ears. Nonetheless, the use of cell phones is not allowed on public transportation and people abide by this rule. On long distance trains you can use your phone in the deck area; otherwise, switch your phone to vibrate or, as they say in Japanese, "manner mode."

The more you speak Japanese on the telephone, the easier it will become. One day, when you find yourself bowing on the phone, you'll know your Japanese is perfect!

Answering the Telephone

When you answer the phone, give either your name or the name of your company or department.

- **Satō desu**　佐藤です　*Sato speaking*
- **Eigyō desu**　営業です　*Sales Department*

If you can't catch what people say, ask them to repeat or speak more slowly.

- **Sumimasen. Mō ichido o-negai-shimasu.**
  すみません。もう一度、お願いします
  I'm sorry. Please say that again.
- **Sumimasen. Yukkuri hanashite kudasai.**
  すみません。ゆっくり話してください
  I'm sorry. Please speak slowly.

When giving phone numbers in Japanese, zero is spoken as **zero** or **rei**, and the word **no** is used to separate the numbers. So this is how you would say the following number for Tokyo:

0　3　–　3　1　2　4　–　5　6　7　8
Rei san no, san ichi ni yon no, go roku nana hachi

Incidentally, the pound key ♯ is pronounced **shāpu** and the star key ＊ **kome-jirushi**, which means "sign for rice" since it looks like 米, the character for rice.

Asking for Someone

3.02

Choose your words according to the person with whom you are speaking. Michael calls his own office and asks for a Japanese colleague. He uses either the surname or, for those higher up in the organisation, name and job title.

- **Moshi moshi, Tērā desu. Satō (Suzuki, Tanaka-buchō), o-negai shimasu.**
  もしもし、テーラーです。佐藤 (鈴木・田中部長) 、お願いします。
  Hello, this is Taylor. Can I speak to Sato (Suzuki, Manager Tanaka)?

When calling another organisation you could say:

- **Shanhai daigaku no Rin desu. Yamada-kyōju o-negai shimasu.**
  上海大学の林です。山田教授お願いします。
  My name is Lin and I'm from Shanghai University. Professor Yamada, please.

But the following, using a humble verb about yourself and an honorific verb about the professor, would be impeccable:

- **Shanhai daigaku no Rin to mōshimasu ga. Yamada-kyōju, irasshaimasu ka?**
  上海大学の林と申しますが、山田教授いらっしゃいますか。
  I'm called Lin and I'm from Shanghai University. Is Professor Yamada there?

On the other hand, if you want to speak to a member of your family, and you're in a situation where you need to be polite, don't forget to refer to him or her with the same humble terms you would use for yourself.

- **Maikeru desu ga, kanai orimasu ka?**
  マイケルですが、家内おりますか。
  This is Michael. Is my wife there?

3.03 Starting a Conversation

These phrases are often used at the start of a telephone conversation:

- **Chotto o-kiki shitain' desu ga.**
  ちょっとお聞きしたいんですが、
  I have an inquiry.

- **Tabi-tabi sumimasen.**
  たびたびすみません。
  Sorry to keep phoning you.

- **O-denwa itadaita sō desu ga.**
  お電話いただいたそうですが。
  I had a message saying you'd called.

- **Saki-hodo wa dōmo.**
  先ほどはどうも。
  Thank you for just now. (Used when phoning people back with the answer, for example, to an inquiry.)

When calling someone's home late at night, many people say:

- **Yabun mōshi-wake arimasen.**
  夜分、申し訳ありません。
  Excuse me for calling this late at night.

3.04

Taking a Call for Someone Else

When the call is for somebody else you can say:

- **Hai, chotto matte kudasai. Satō-san, denwa haitte imasu.**
  はい、ちょっと待ってください。佐藤さん、電話入っています。
  Please wait a moment. Ms Sato, there's a call for you.

- **Shitsurei desu ga, dochira-sama deshō ka?**
  失礼ですが、どちらさまでしょうか。
  Excuse me, but may I ask who is calling?

If the person can't get to the phone, say one of the following:

- **Sumimasen ga, rusu desu / dekakete orimasu.**
  すみませんが、留守です ／ 出かけております。
  I'm sorry but she's not here / she's gone out.

- **Ima seki o hazushite imasu.**
  今、席をはずしています。
  She's not at her desk right now.

- **Denwa-chū desu / Kaigi-chū desu / Raikyaku-chū desu / Jugyō-chū desu.**
  電話中です ／ 会議中です ／ 来客中です ／ 授業中です。
  She's on another line / She's in a meeting / She's got a visitor / She's in class.

Leaving a Message

If the person you want to speak with is not in, ask if you can leave a message.

- **Denwa ga atta koto o o-tsutae kudasai. Mata o-denwa shimasu.**
  電話があったことをお伝えください。また、お電話します。
  Tell him I called. I'll call back later.

- **Dengon, o-negai dekimasu ka?**
  伝言、お願いできますか。
  Can I leave a message?

- **O-tesuki no toki ni, orikaeshi o-denwa kudasai.**
  お手すきのときに、折り返しお電話ください。
  Please ask her to call as soon as she's free.

- **Owarimashitara, watashi ni denwa o suru yō ni o-tsutae ku-dasai.**
  終わりましたら、私に電話をするようにお伝えください。
  When he's through, ask him to telephone me.

Using Your Cell Phone

Here are some phrases you might need when using your cell phone.

- **Shitsurei shimasu. Chotto denwa ni demasu no de. Sumima-sen.**
  失礼します。ちょっと電話に出ますので。すみません。
  Excuse me. Do you mind if I take this call? I'm very sorry.

- **O-matase shimashita. Ima no denwa o matte ita mono desu kara. Kanai (byōin, kaisha, kaigai) kara deshita. Taihen shitsurei shimashita.**
  お待たせしました。今の電話を待っていたものですから。家内（病院・会社・海外）からでした。たいへん失礼しました。
  Sorry to keep you waiting. I was expecting that call from my wife (hospital, company, overseas). I do apologize.

- **Sumimasen. Dōshitemo denai to ikenai denwa ga ima hairimashita. Sugu kakenaoshimasu.**
  すみません。どうしても出ないといけない電話が今入りました。すぐ、掛けなおします。
  I'm sorry. A call has just come in that I have to answer. I'll call you right back.

- **Amari nagaku hanashi wa dekinai! Batterii ga kiresō.**
  あまり長く話しはできない！バッテリーが切れそう。
  I can't talk long! My batteries are low (about to go dead).

- **Moshi moshi, kikoemasu ka? Denpa no tōi tokoro ni iru no yo.**
  もしもし、聞こえますか。電波の遠いところにいるのよ。
  Hello? Can you hear me? The reception here is poor.

- **Denwa ga togirete, yoku kikoenain' da kedo.**
  話が途切れて、よく聞こえないんだけど。
  You're breaking up. I can't hear you very well.

As stated earlier, people don't use phones on public transport. You'll hear this message on trains and at the cinema, concerts, meetings etc.

- **Keitai denwa no dengen o kiru ka manā mōdo ni kirikaete kudasai.**
  携帯電話の電源を切るかマナーモードに切り替えてください。
  Please switch off your mobile phone, or switch to vibrate (manner mode).

3.07 Buying a Phone

It's hard to make sense of all the different contracts, but Lin knows what phone he wants and it seems to be a good deal.

LIN:

Sumimasen. Kono denwa wa ¥0 to natte imasu ga, donna shikumi desu ka.

すみません。この電話は¥0となっていますが、どんな仕組みですか。

Excuse me. It says this phone is ¥0 but how is that worked out?

SHOP ASSISTANT:

Kishu daikin wa nijūyon-kai no bunkatsu-barai desu. Maitsuki no o-shiharai ni fukumarete imasu.

機種代金は24回の分割払いです。毎月のお支払いに含まれています。

The payment for the handset is in 24 installments. It's included in the monthly payments.

LIN:

Maitsuki, ikura haraeba ii desu ka.

毎月、いくら払えばいいですか。

How much would I have to pay every month?

SHOP ASSISTANT:

Kono puran no baai, maitsuki no kihon shiyōryō wa 5,000 en, kishu daikin wa 1,920 en, soshite ninenkan no waribiki 1,920 en ga arimasu no de, maitsuki no o-shiharai wa 5,000 en desu. Ato, tsūwaryō ga arimasu.

このプランの場合、毎月の基本使用料は5,000円、機種代金は1,920円、そして2年間の割引1,920円がありますので、毎月のお支払いは5,000円です。後、通話料があります。

In the case of this plan, the monthly charge for use of the phone is 5,000 yen, the payment for the handset is 1,920 yen, then there's a discount of 1,920 for two years, so every month you pay 5,000 yen. Then there's the cost of the calls.

LIN:

Tsūwaryō wa ikura desu ka?
通話料はいくらですか。
How much do calls cost?

SHOP ASSISTANT:

Sanjūbyō ni nijūichi en desu.
30秒に21円です。
21 yen for 30 seconds.

LIN:

Kaigai de tsukaemasu ka?
海外で使えますか。
Can I use it abroad?

SHOP ASSISTANT:

Kaigai de tsukaeba, kono kaigai teigaku puran o o-susume shimasu.
海外で使えば、この海外定額プランをお勧めします。
If you use it abroad, I recommend this plan for an overseas fixed charge.

LIN:

Iroiro mite kita ga, kore ga ii rashii ne. Kore ni shimasu.
いろいろ見てきたが、これがいいらしいね。これにします。
I've seen various ones but this seems good. I'll go for this one.

SHOP ASSISTANT:

Arigatō gozaimasu. O-mōshikomi no sai, gaikokujin tōroku shōmeisho to pasupōto ga hitsuyō desu ga.

ありがとうございます。お申し込みの際、外国人登録証明書とパスポートが必要ですが。

Thank you. When you apply, you'll need your alien registration certificate and your passport.

LIN:

Motte imasu yo. Tetsuzuki o shimashō.

持っていますよ。手続きをしましょう。

I've got them. Let's do the paperwork.

3.08 Asking for Directions

Now that he's got his phone, Lin goes to visit his friend Takuya but finds himself hopelessly lost and returns to the station. He calls his friend for help.

LIN:

Rin da. Okurete gomen. Michi ga wakaranakute.

林だ。遅れてごめん。道が分からなくて、

This is Lin. Sorry to be late but I can't find the way.

TAKUYA:

Ima, doko?

今、どこ?

Where are you now?

LIN:

Eki no kaisatsuguchi ni modottan' desu yo. Minamiguchi.

駅の改札口に戻ったんですよ。南口。

I've come back to the ticket barrier at the station. The South exit.

TAKUYA:

**Ja ne, yakkyoku mieru? Yakkyoku no kado o hidari ni ma-
gatte, massugu ni kite. Tokyo Ginko no ura dakedo, mukae ni
dete iku kara.**

じゃね、薬局、見える?薬局の角を左に曲がって、まっすぐ
に来て。東京銀行の裏だけど、迎えに出ていくから。

*Let me see, can you see a pharmacy? Turn left at the corner where
the pharmacy is and then go straight. We're behind the Tokyo
Bank but I'll come out and meet you.*

LIN:

Wakatta. Ja ne.

分かった。じゃね。

OK. See you soon.

3.09 Calling in Sick

Max calls his Japanese boss. Note that the boss uses informal men's
speech while Max maintains a more formal style.

BOSS:

Okada desu.

岡田です。

Okada speaking.

MAX:

Makkusu desu.

マックスです。

It's Max.

BOSS:

Yā! Dō shita?

ヤー。どうした。

Hi! What's the matter?

MAX:

Jitsu wa, atama ga itakute, kyō ichi-nichi yasumasete ita-dakitain' desu ga.

実は、頭が痛くて、今日一日休ませていただきたいんですが、

Well, I've got a terrible headache, and I'd like to take the day off.

BOSS:

Sore wa komatta na. Kyō kimi no kawari ni naru hito ga inai no de, nantoka dete korarenai kana?

それは困ったな。今日、君の代わりになる人がいないので、何とか出てこられないかな。

Oh, no. I've got no one to replace you today. Can't you somehow make it in?

MAX:

Atama ga gangan shite, muri desu ne.

頭ががんがんして、無理ですね。

My head really hurts. It's out of the question.

BOSS:

Sō ka. Ja, shikata nai ne. Muri shinai hō ga ii yo. O-daiji ni.

そうか。じゃ、仕方ないね。無理しない方がいいよ。お大事に。

I see. Well, it can't be helped. You'd better not overdo it. Take care of yourself.

MAX:

Mōshi-wake arimasen. Shitsurei shimasu.

申し訳ありません。失礼します。

I'm really sorry. Goodbye.

3.10 Making an Appointment

The language used in business can be very formal. In this dialogue Michael makes an appointment with a client.

MICHAEL:

Moshi-moshi. Takahashi-buchō de irasshaimasu ka?
もしもし、高橋部長でいらっしゃいますか。
Hello? Is that Mr. Takahashi? (lit. Division Manager Takahashi)

TAKAHASHI:

Hai, sō desu.
はいそうです。
Yes, speaking.

MICHAEL:

Ecoshisutemu no Tērā de gozaimasu. Ohayō gozaimasu.
エコシステムのテーラーでございます。お早うございます。
This is Taylor of EcoSystems. Good morning.

TAKAHASHI:

Ohayō gozaimasu. Itsumo o-sewa ni natte orimasu.
お早うございます。いつもお世話になっております。
Good morning. We're very much obliged to you.

MICHAEL:

Kochira koso. Jitsu wa, buchō no go-tsugō o kikimashite, aite iru jikan ni demo o-ukagai dekitara to omoimashite.
こちらこそ。実は、部長のご都合を聞きまして、空いている時間にでもお伺いできたらと思いまして、
On the contrary (we are obliged to you). Well, I'm calling because I'd like to come and see you and I wonder when would be convenient.

TAKAHASHI:

A sō desu ka? Go-yōken wa nan' desu ka?

ア、そうですか。ご用件は何ですか。

I see. What's it about?

MICHAEL:

Hai. Watakushi-domo no atarashii shōene shōhin no koto o go-setsumei ni agaritai no desu ga.

はい、私どもの新しい省エネ商品のことをご説明に上がりたいのですが、

I d like to come and tell you about our new energy saving product.

TAKAHASHI:

Kekkō desu yo. Itsugoro ga yoroshii desu ka?

結構ですよ。いつごろがよろしいですか。

All right. When would be convenient?

MICHAEL:

Sō desu ne. Dochira ka to iu to, ashita ka asatte, hayai hō ga iin' desu ga.

そうですね。どちらかというと、明日かあさって、早い方がいいんですが、

Let me see. I would prefer tomorrow or the day after; the sooner the better.

TAKAHASHI:

Ē-to, sō shimasu to, ashita no gogo nara orimasu.

えーと、そうしますと、明日の午後ならおります。

Let's see. I'll be here tomorrow afternoon.

MICHAEL:

Sore-dewa, ashita ni-ji goro ukagatte mo yoroshii deshō ka?

それでは、明日二時ごろ伺ってもよろしいでしょうか。

Then may I come around two o'clock tomorrow?

TAKAHASHI:

Kekkō desu. Ashita no gogo, ni-ji, o-machi shite orimasu.

結構です。明日の午後二時、お待ちしております。

That's fine. I'll be waiting for you at two tomorrow afternoon.

MICHAEL:

Arigatō gozaimasu. Sore de wa, o-ukagai itashimasu. Yoro-shiku o-negai shimasu. Shitsurei shimasu.

ありがとうございます。それでは、お伺いいたします。よろし
くお願いいたします。失礼いたします。

*Thank you. Well then, I'll visit you. I look forward to seeing you.
Goodbye.*

 3.11

Changing an Appointment

Having managed so well to get this appointment, Michael now finds
he has to reschedule it.

MICHAEL:

**Tērā desu ga, sakihodo wa dōmo arigatō gozaimashita. Jitsu
wa, o-yakusoku itadaita no desu ga, ashita kyū na yōken de
Ōsaka e iku koto ni narimashite, hontō ni mōshi-wake arimasen ga, asatte ni nobashite itadakenai deshō ka?**

テーラーですが、先ほどはどうもありがとうございました。
実は、お約束いただいたのですが、明日急な用件で大阪へ
行くことになりまして、本当に申し訳ありませんが、あさって
に延ばしていただけないでしょうか。

*This is Taylor again. It's about our appointment. It turns out that I
have to go to Osaka tomorrow on urgent business. Would it be possible to postpone the appointment until the day after tomorrow?*

3.12 Calling Directory Assistance

Dial 104 for directory assistance. There's a small fee but it's a useful service.

OPERATOR:

Bangō annai desu.
番号案内です。
Directory assistance.

KIM:

Moshi moshi. Kankoku Kōkū wa nanban deshō ka?
もしもし。韓国航空は何番でしょうか。
Hello. What number is Korean Airways?

OPERATOR:

Hai. O-machi kudasaimase. Yoyaku de yoroshii deshō ka?
はい、お待ちくださいませ。予約でよろしいでしょうか。
One moment please. Do you want reservations?

KIM:

Hai, yoyaku, o-negai shimasu.
はい、予約お願いします。
Yes, reservations please.

OPERATOR:

De wa, go-annai itashimasu. * * * O-matase itashimashita. Sono kata wa rei-san no, san-hachi-ichi-ichi no, nana-ichi-rei-roku desu. Arigatō gozaimashita.
では、ご案内いたします。＊＊＊ お待たせいたしました。その方は03-3811-7106です。ありがとうございました。
Here is the information, (recording) Sorry to have kept you waiting. The number is 03-3811-7106. Thank you.

Phoning Emergency Services

3.13

To telephone the police, dial 110. This emergency number is known as **hyaku tōban**. For fires and situations requiring an ambulance, dial 119. (Note that if you want to be treated by a particular hospital, you might be better telephoning that hospital for an ambulance or finding your own way there.) In this conversation, Lin has just dialed 119 to call an ambulance for his friend who has suddenly collapsed.

FIRE/AMBULANCE SERVICE:

Kyūkyūtai desu.
救急隊です。
Emergency.

LIN:

Kyūkyūsha, o-negai shimasu.
救急車、お願いします。
I need an ambulance.

FIRE/AMBULANCE SERVICE:

Hai. Dō shimashita ka?
はい。どうしましたか。
OK. What's happened?

LIN:

Tomodachi ga taorete, ishiki-fumei desu!
友達が倒れて、意識不明です。
My friend's lying unconscious!

FIRE/AMBULANCE SERVICE:

Ochitsuite, o-namae to jūsho o dōzo.
落ち着いて、お名前と住所をどうぞ。
Keep calm and give me your name and address.

LIN:

Rin desu. Tomodachi no jūsho wa Nishi-machi ni no yon no san, Famiri Kōpo desu.

林です。友達の住所は西町2—4—3、ファミリコーポです。

My name's Lin. My friend's address is Family Co-op, Nishimachi 2 – 4 – 3.

FIRE/AMBULANCE SERVICE:

Mejirushi ni naru yō na mono o itte kudasai.

目印になるようなものを言ってください。

Please tell me if there are any landmarks.

LIN:

Tokyo Ginkō no ura desu.

東京銀行の裏です。

It's behind the Tokyo Bank.

FIRE/AMBULANCE SERVICE:

Hai. Sugu ikimasu.

はい、すぐ行きます。

We'll be right there.

Here are a few more phrases for emergencies. The first concerns the fire department, the next two, the police.

- **Ie ga kaji desu. Sugu kite kudasai.**
  家が家事です。すぐ来てください。
  The house is on fire. Come immediately.

- **Fushin na hito ga ie no mae de uro-uro shite imasu.**
  不審な人が家の前でうろうろしています。
  There's a suspicious person loitering in front of our house.

- **Tonari de bōryoku o furutte'ru mitai desu.**
  隣で暴力をふるってるみたいです。
  There seems to be a fight going on next door.

3.14 Some Phone Numbers

104	Directory enquiries
106	Collect calls
113	Telephone repairs
110	Police (**hyaku tōban**)
119	Fire/ambulance service (**hyaku jūkyūban**)
177	Weather (or area code + 177)
117	Time
171	Message recording service for use in disasters
(03) 5774-0992	Tokyo English Lifeline (TELL)

3.15 Words and Expressions

keitai	携帯	*cell phone*
denwa suru, denwa o kakeru	電話する、電話を掛ける	*to telephone*
rusuden o saisei suru	留守伝を再生する	*play back recorded messages*
mēru	メール	*messages*
manā mōdo	マナーモード	*sound off, vibrate (manner mode)*
denwachō	電話帳	*address book, contacts (cell phone) telephone directory*
denwa o kiru	電話を切る	*to hang up*
denwa ga kireta	電話が切れた	*The line has gone dead*

denwa ga tōi	電話が遠い	*I can't hear you very well (We have a bad connection).*
jūden suru	充電する	*to charge (battery)*
denwa bangō	電話番号	*telephone number*
kōshū denwa	公衆電話	*public telephone*
kyokuban	局番	*area code*
kokusai denwa	国際電話	*international call*
machigai denwa	間違い電話	*wrong number*
itazura denwa, meiwaku denwa	いたずら電話・迷惑電話	*obscene/prank telephone call*
dekome	デコメ	*"decorated mail," animated decorations for keitai messages and blogs*

Chapter 4 Traveling

Traveling

Traditional japanese hospitality, a safe and secure environment, no tipping, and a hugely reliable transportation system make travelling in Japan reasonably trouble-free. But make sure you get the timing right. Avoid the peak periods of New Year, Golden Week and the Bon Festival when trains and accommodation need to be booked months in advance and roads are heavily congested. Choose the season carefully too.

The best times are May and November, when the weather is settled and temperatures comfortable. In May the cherry blossoms are over but azaleas and fresh green leaves abound. In November red maples are stunning against clear blue skies. Sightseeing in the summer is physically demanding. With temperatures over 85°F/30°C and high humidity you'll need to pace yourself, allowing extra time for stops in air conditioned coffee shops, etc. At least the sights won't be crowded. Winters are severe in the north of the country and in the mountains—although winter sports and festivals have their attractions.

Obviously you should book ahead in peak season. Sightseers crowd the tourist areas and huge groups of schoolchildren tour the famous sights in spring and fall. Especially when the cherry blossoms are in flower or when the autumn colors reach their peak, accommodation even for weekdays may be hard to find in popular tourist places like Kyoto.

If you're visiting from abroad, get a Japan Rail Pass, an excellent deal but only available to visitors on a tourist visa. It not only gives you unlimited travel on the rail network (including the bullet trains) for periods of one, two, or three weeks but also dispenses with the troublesome task of buying tickets. They cannot be purchased in Japan, so buy the voucher before you leave home.

If you don't have a rail pass, you'll need to familiarize yourself with the system for buying tickets and making reservations. The passenger ticket (**jōshaken**) is all you need to travel on subways, commuter trains, and non-express trains. But if you travel long distance on express trains like the bullet trains, you'll also need to buy an "express" ticket (**tokkyūken**). With these two tickets, you board the cars marked **jiyūseki** (unreserved) and sit in any available seat. You can also pay a small extra charge to reserve a seat in a reserved carriage or a hefty surcharge to travel in luxury in the "green car." Much cheaper are long distance buses, which can be booked on the internet.

Another boon for travellers to Japan is the coin locker. Located at stations everywhere, for a few hundred yen you can dump your baggage for the day and travel lightly. When planning your trip, consider bringing several bags that you can pack into a coin locker, rather than a suitcase.

There's a wide range of accommodation to choose from and you can find information and make bookings on the internet. You can stay at a regular hotel, or a **ryokan**, a Japanese inn where you sleep on **futon** bedding laid out on the **tatami** mats after dinner. As a rule, breakfast and dinner are included in the price, which is calculated per person, although things are changing and in some places you may be able to eat out.

Cheaper alternatives include the **minshuku**, a family-run guesthouse, and the **penshon** (from the French, **pension**) where sleeping is in beds, and dinner and breakfast are usually Western-style. Another option is the business hotel. Although lacking in character, they provide a clean bed at a reasonable price and, since meals are not included, they offer you more flexibility for scheduling your time.

You might be intrigued by the idea of staying at one of the many temples nationwide that allow a traveler to stay overnight (**shukubō**). Besides offering a glimpse into Buddhist life, these temples are often oases of quiet. Some temples specialize in serving vegan temple cuisine; others may offer a simple meal.

And finally, there are youth hostels, which are very reasonable, but you might have to apply well in advance.

Traditionally many people's idea of a good rest is a few days away from it all at a rustic hot spring (**onsen**). Because the different minerals in the water are recommended for various, often chronic, ailments, people used to spend several weeks at a hot spring. In recent times, an overnight stay, often in a group, is more common. Many people bathe from three to five times during an overnight stay.

Some **ryokan** allow non-guests use of the bath during the day, either just the bath or a package that includes lunch and the use of a room for a few hours. So if you are caught on a cold and rainy day, why not give up on sightseeing and take a soothing bath instead?

There's no great mystique about onsen etiquette: just sit on a stool and scrub yourself thoroughly before you try the different baths. Be warned though, some places haven't caught up with the fashion for tattooes, and you could be asked to leave as a suspected yakuza! If this applies to you, cover up.

Riding Subways and Trains

4.01

If you cannot read the fare tables for riding subways or commuter trains, buy the cheapest ticket and pay the difference at the fare adjustment machine when you reach your destination. Ask for the platform you want like this:

> • **Sumimasen. Shinjuku-yuki wa nanban-sen desu ka?**
> すみません。新宿行きは何番線ですか。
> *Excuse me. From what platform can I get the train headed for Shinjuku?*

On the platform, to make sure you are waiting for the right train, you can go up to a passenger or a station official and ask:

> • **Ochanomizu de tomarimasu ka?**
> 御茶ノ水で止まりますか。
> *Does this train stop at Ochanomizu?*

When you reach your stop in a crowded train, push your way to the exit while saying:

> • **Sumimasen. Orimasu.**
> すみません。降ります。
> *Excuse me! I'm getting off!*

4.02 Buying Express Train Tickets

You can book tickets online (in several languages) or buy tickets at machines, which have an English language option. If you're stuck, stand in line to speak to a representative.

KIM:

Tsugi no hikari de Kyōto made ichimai kudasai.
次のヒカリで京都まで一枚ください。
One ticket to Tokyo on the next Hikari bullet train, please.

TICKET SELLER:

Man'in desu ne. Nijū-roppun nara seki ga arimasu ga.
満員ですね。26分なら席がありますが、
The train's full. But there are seats on the (one leaving at) twenty-six minutes past.

KIM:

Jā, o-negai shimasu.
じゃ、お願いします。
OK. I'll take that.

TICKET SELLER:

Jōshaken mo?
乗車券も？
Do you want a passenger ticket as well?

KIM:

Hai.
はい。
Yes.

TICKET SELLER:

Kaeri no kippu wa dō shimasu ka?
帰りの切符はどうしますか。
What do you want to do about a return ticket?

KIM:

Kaeri no jikan ga mada wakaranai no de, jiyūseki ni shite kudasai.

帰りの時間がまだ分かないので、自由席にしてください。

I don't know yet what time I'll be returning, so make it unreserved.

TICKET SELLER:

Sore de wa, iki no jōshaken, tokkyūken, shiteiseki. Kaeri no jōshaken to tokkyūken. Zenbu de niman rokusen-en ni narimasu.

それでは、行きの乗車券、特急券、指定席。帰りの乗車券と特急券。全部で26,000円になります。

So, for the outgoing journey (here is) the passenger ticket, the express ticket and a reserved seat. For the return, the passenger ticket and the express ticket. That will be 26,000 yen.

4.03   Canceling a Train Reservation

There's a small charge for canceling a reservation at least two days before the train leaves, more if you wait until later.

- **Jūichi-nichi, gozen ku-ji no Hiroshima-yuki no Nozomi o yoyaku shitan' desu ga, kyanseru shinakereba naranai no de, harai-modoshi ga dekimasu ka?**

  11日午前9時、広島行きののぞみを予約したんですが、キャンセルしなければならないので、払い戻しができますか。

  I have reservations for the Nozomi bullet train on the eleventh at 9 in the morning, but I have to cancel it. Can I get a refund?

4.04 Missing a Train

If you miss your train, ask a station official if you can ride the next train.

- **Ressha ni noriokurete shimatta. Kono kippu nara tsugi ni noremasu ka?**
  列車に乗り遅れてしまった。この切符なら、次に乗れますか。
  I missed the train. Can I go on the next train with these tickets?

4.05 On the Train

Once you've boarded the train, find a seat and get something to eat and drink. Don't miss out on the **bentō** or lunch boxes. Traditionally each station had its own speciality, the **ekiben**, and it's fun to try them out. The **makunouchi** (*lit.* lunch to eat in the interval) has a long history and consists of white rice with titbits of grilled fish, omelette and vegetables.

- **Aite'masu ka?**
  空いてますか。
  Is this seat free?

- **Sumimasen. Hotto futatsu kudasai.**
  すみません。ホット二つください。
  Excuse me. Two hot coffees, please.

- **O-cha to o-bentō kudasai. Dō iu mono, aru ka na?**
  お茶とお弁当ください。どういうもの、あるかな。
  Green tea and a box lunch, please. What kind do you have?

- **Makunouchi toka, tonkatsu toka. Unagi, o-sushi. Iro iro arimasu.**
  幕の内とか、とんかつとか。うなぎ、おすし。いろいろあります。
  Mixed selection and fried pork cutlet. Grilled eel, sushi. All kinds.

4.06 Renting a Car

If you use one of the big national companies, you can make a reservation on the internet (in Japanese) or phone in English. Travel agents and the train companies also offer good deals on car rentals. Max goes along to a company near his home.

MAX:

Konnichiwa. Tōka, jūichi-nichi, futsukakan kuruma o karitain' desu ga.
こんにちは。10日、11日、二日間、車を借りたいんですが、
Hi. I'd like to rent a car for two days, the 10th and 11th.

SALES STAFF:

Hai. Shashu wa nani ga ii desu ka. Sen cc no kogatasha, D-kurasu da to, ryōkin wa ichinichi rokusen yonhyaku-en, sono ue no E-kurasu da to nanasen-en. Zenhoshō-tsuki desu ga, anshin kōsu o o-susume shimasu.
はい。車種は何がいいですか。千ccの小型車、Dクラスだと、料金は1日6,400円、その上のEクラスだと7,000円。全保障つきですが、安心コースをおすすめします。
All right. What kind of car would you like? A 1,000 cc small car, the D-class is 6,400 yen a day and the one above that, the E-class, is 7,000 yen. All insurance is included but I do recommend our "peace of mind" course.

MAX:

Kānabi wa tsuite imasu ka?
カーナビはついていますか。
Is there GPS in the car?

SALES STAFF:

Tsuite imasu yo,
ついていますよ。
Yes, there is.

MAX:

Sore de wa, D-kurasu no kuruma, hoken wa anshin kōsu ni shimasu.
それでは、Dクラスの車、保険は安心コースにします。
Well, I'll take a D-class car, and for the insurance I'll go for the "peace of mind" course.

SALES STAFF:

Arigatō gozaimasu. Nihon no menkyoshō ga nakute mo ii desu. Kokusai menkyo de kekkō desu. Shikashi, kurejitto kādo no maebarai ga hitsuyō desu.
ありがとうございます。日本の免許証がなくてもいいです。国際免許で結構です。しかし、クレジットカードの前払いが必要です。
Thank you. We don't need a Japanese driving license. Your international driving licence is fine. But you'll need to pay in advance on your credit card.

4.07

Asking for Road Directions

Secondary roads are not always marked on road maps, and road signs can be inadequate or lost in a jungle of wires, posts, placards, and shrubbery. Max gets lost and drops in at a convenience store to ask for directions.

MAX:

Sumimasen. Kōsoku no iriguchi e wa kore de iin' desu ka?
すみません。高速の入り口へはこれでいいんですか。
Excuse me. Is this the way to the Expressway?

STORE STAFF:

Iya. Iki-sugi desu ne. Sō ne, temae no ōkina kōsaten ni mo-dotte, migi e magatte, san-kiro gurai iku to, kōsoku no iriguchi ga mieru hazu desu yo.
いや、行きすぎですね。そうね、手前の大きな交差点に戻って、右へ曲がって、そこから3キロぐらい行くと、高速の入り口が見えるはずですよ。
No. You've gone too far. Let me see, go back to the last big inter-section and turn right. After about three kilometres, you should see the entrance to the expressway.

MAX:

Arigatō gozaimashita.
ありがとうございました。
Thank you very much.

4.08 Calling for Help

Max is ill-fated. On his way home he has trouble with the car and needs to ring the rental company's helpline.

CALL CENTER:

Nihon Rentakā desu.
日本レンタカーです。
Hello. This is Japan Rentacar.

MAX:

Sukiijō de batterii ga agatchatta. Dō shitara ii desu ka.
スキー場でバッテリーが上がちゃった。どうしたらいいですか。
My car battery's gone dead at the ski slope. What should I do?

CALL CENTER:

Hai. O-namae to basho, kuruma no nanbā, o-negai shimasu.
はい。お名前と場所、車のナンバー、お願いします。
OK. Please give me your name, your location, and the car number.

MAX:

Basho wa Zaō sukiijō no chūshajō no iriguchi de, namae wa Buraun, kuruma no nanbā wa Sendai rokujūyon no rokujū desu.
場所は蔵王スキー場の駐車場の入り口で、名前はブラウン、車のナンバーは仙台64—60です。
I'm at the entrance to the parking lot of the Zao ski slope, the name is Brown, and the car registration number is Sendai 64-60.

CALL CENTER:

Hai, wakarimashita.Yonjippun gurai de tantōsha ga ikimasu no de, sono mama o-machi kudasai.

はい、分かりました。40分ぐらいで担当者が行きますので、そのままお待ちください。

I see. Someone should be with you in about forty minutes. Please wait.

MAX:

O-negai shimasu.

お願いします。

OK. Thank you.

More words to describe common car problems:

- **Gasorin ga kireta.**
  ガソリンが切れた。
  I've run out of gas.

- **Enjin ga koshō shita.**
  エンジンが故障した。
  I'm having engine trouble.

- **Kagi o ireta mama rokku shite shimatta.**
  鍵を入れたままロックしてしまった。
  I've locked the keys inside the car.

- **Sharin ga sokkō ni ochite shimatta.**
  車輪がそっこうに落ちてしまった。
  One wheel is stuck in the ditch.

4.09 Planning a Trip

You can make your travel plans and do much of the booking on the internet. A lot of sites are in English, but here's an example of a Japanese site (more information on using the internet in the chapter on Shopping).

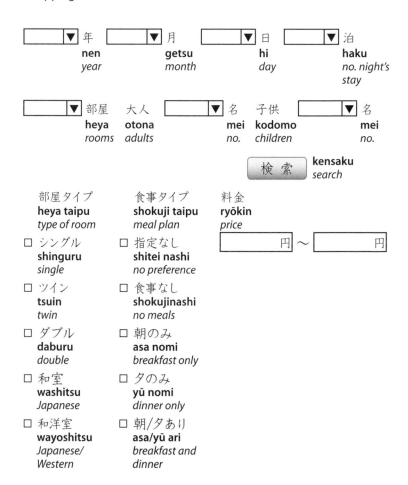

▼ 年	▼ 月	▼ 日	▼ 泊
nen *year*	**getsu** *month*	**hi** *day*	**haku** *no. night's stay*

▼ 部屋	大人	▼ 名	子供	▼ 名
heya *rooms*	**otona** *adults*	**mei** *no.*	**kodomo** *children*	**mei** *no.*

検索 **kensaku** *search*

部屋タイプ
heya taipu
type of room

☐ シングル
shinguru
single

☐ ツイン
tsuin
twin

☐ ダブル
daburu
double

☐ 和室
washitsu
Japanese

☐ 和洋室
wayoshitsu
Japanese/ Western

食事タイプ
shokuji taipu
meal plan

☐ 指定なし
shitei nashi
no preference

☐ 食事なし
shokujinashi
no meals

☐ 朝のみ
asa nomi
breakfast only

☐ 夕のみ
yū nomi
dinner only

☐ 朝/夕あり
asa/yū ari
breakfast and dinner

料金
ryōkin
price

[　　　] 円 〜 [　　　] 円

4.10 Confirming a Room Reservation

As your trip approaches, you might like to confirm that your internet booking has gone through.

RECEPTIONIST:

Ichinoyu de gozaimasu.
一の湯でございます。
This is Ichinoyu.

LIN:

Anō, intānetto de, nijūroku-nichi ippaku o yoyaku shimashi-ta ga, kakunin shite moratte ii desu ka. Rin to mōshimasu.
あのう、インターネットで、26日一泊を予約しましたが、確認してもらっていいですか。林と申します。
Er, I made a reservation on the internet for one night on the 26ᵗʰ. Could you confirm it please? My name is Li.

RECEPTIONIST:

Hai. Nimei-sama desu ne. Go-tōchaku wa nanjigoro ni narisō desu ka?
はい。2名さまですね。ご到着は何時ごろになりそうですか。
That's fine. Two people. About what time are you likely to arrive?

LIN:

Sō desu ne. Machi o mite mawatte kara ikimasu no de, roku-ji-goro ni narisō ka na.
そうですね、町を見て回ってから行きますので、6時ごろになりそうかな。
Let me see. We'll go after we've looked around the town, so it will probably be around six.

RECEPTIONIST:

O-machi shite orimasu. O-ki o tsukete o-dekake kudasai.
お待ちしております。お気をつけてお出かけください。
We'll be waiting for you. Please take care on your way here.

4.11　Asking the Way

You'll find people are more than happy to give you directions.

- **Sumimasen. Inarimon wa dochira desu ka.**
  すみません。いなり門はどちらですか。
  Excuse me. Which way to the Inarimon Gate [of the Asakusa Kannon Temple]?

- **Sumimasen. Daiichi Hoteru o sagashite imasu ga.**
  すみません。第一ホテルを探していますが。
  Excuse me. I'm looking for the Daiichi Hotel.

- **Miyajima e dono yō ni ittara ii desu ka? Ressha ga ii desu ka? Romen densha ga ii desu ka? Soretomo fune de itta hō ga ii desu ka?**
  宮島へどのように行ったらいいですか。列車がいいですか。路面電車がいいですか。それとも船で行った方がいいですか。
  How should we go to Miyajima? By train? By tram? Or would it be better to go by boat?

4.12 Asking Where to Go

Ask at tourist information or your lodging about places to visit and places to eat.

LIN:

Chotto o-kiki shimasu ga, chikaku no meisho o oshiete kudasai.

ちょっとお聞きしますが、近くの名所を教えてください。

May I ask you a question? Can you tell me the places of interest nearby?

RECEPTIONIST:

Hai. O-shiro ga yūmei desu yo. Saiken shita mono desu ga, naka ni subarashii hakubutsukan ga arimasu.

はい。お城が有名ですよ。再建したものですが、中にすばらしい博物館があります。

All right. The castle is famous. It's a reconstruction but there's a superb museum inside.

LIN:

Dentōteki na mingeihin o utte iru mise nado wa arimasen ka?

伝統的な民芸品を売っている店などはありませんか。

Are there any shops or such like selling traditional craft items?

RECEPTIONIST:

Takusan arimasu yo. Chōchin o tsukuttari, senbei o yaitari suru omoshiroi mise ga takusan arimasu.

たくさんありますよ。ちょうちんを作ったり、せんべいを焼いたりする面白い店がたくさんあります。

There are lots. There are lots of interesting shops making paper lanterns, baking rice crackers.

LIN:

> **Sugoi na. Basho o oshiete kudasai. Sore kara, mō hitotsu. Chikaku ni o-susume no resutoran/izakaya wa arimasu ka?**
> すごいな。場所を教えてください。それから、もう一つ。近くにおすすめのレストラン/居酒屋はありますか。
> *Great. Please tell me where they are. And one more thing. Is there a restaurant/bar nearby you can recommend?*

4.13 Using the In-house Telephone

If you're staying at a **ryokan, minshuku,** or **penshon,** you should arrive by about five o'clock because dinner is usually served around six. Japanese hotels and **ryokan** generally supply cotton sleeping kimono, soap, razors, toothbrushes, and toothpaste. Hotels usually provide Western-style bath towels but **ryokan** may not.

Near the phone in the room, there should be a telephone guide that looks something like this:

9	**furonto**	フロント	*front desk*
0	**gaisen**	外線	*outside line*
7	**kyaku-shitsu**	客室	*other guest rooms*
6	**rūmu sābisu**	ルームサービス	*room service*

If you need something, telephone either the front desk or room service.

> • **Moshi-moshi. Sanbyakusan gōshitsu desu ga, kōri/ōkina yukata/rāmen o motte kite kudasai.**
> もしもし。303号室ですが / 氷 / 大きなゆかた / ラーメンを持ってきてください。
> *Hello? This is room 303. Can you bring some ice/a large cotton kimono/a bowl of noodles?*

- **Ekusutora-beddo, o-negai shimashita ga, heya ni wa mada haitte imasen.**
  エクストラベッド、お願いしましたが、部屋にはまだ入っていません。
  We ordered an extra bed, but it's not in the room yet.

- **Ashita no asa wa yōshoku, o-negai dekimasu ka?**
  明日の朝は洋食、お願いできますか。
  For tomorrow morning, can we have Western-style breakfasts?

4.14   The Hot Spring

If you find yourself in a hot spring resort, here are some phrases to get the most out of your experience.

- **Sumimasen. Shukuhaku de wa naku, higaeri de onsen ni hairemasu ka?**
  すみません。宿泊ではなく、日帰りで温泉に入れますか。
  Excuse me. We're not staying the night but may we take the hot spring during the day?

- **Koko no onsen wa nani ni kikimasu ka?**
  ここの温泉は何に効きますか。
  What is this hot spring good for?

- **Ichō no byōki/ryūmachi/yōtsū/hifu-byō ni yoku kikimasu yo.**
  胃腸の病気・リュウマチ・腰痛・皮膚病によく効きますよ。
  It's very good for stomach disorders/rheumatism/ backache/skin diseases.

- **Chotto umete ii desu ka?**
  ちょっとうめていいですか。
  Do you mind if I add a bit of cold water?

4.15   Public Holidays in Japan

This is the calendar for public holidays. When a holiday falls on a Sunday, the following Monday becomes a holiday. If you can, avoid traveling in peak periods: the New Year period (December 29 to January 4), Golden Week (April 29 to May 5), and the Bon Festival (August 13 to 16).

January 1	**ganjitsu**	元日	*New Year's Day*
January 15	**seijin no hi**	成人の日	*Coming of Age Day*
February 11	**kenkoku kinenbi**	建国記念日	*National Founding Day*
March 21	**shunbun no hi**	春分の日	*Spring Equinox Day*
April 29	**midori no hi**	緑の日	*Greenery Day*
May 3	**kenpō kinenbi**	憲法記念日	*Constitution Day*
May 4	**kokumin no kyūjitsu**	国民の休日	*National Holiday*
May 5	**kodomo no hi**	子供の日	*Children's Day*
July 18	**umi no hi**	海の日	*Sea Day*

September 19	**keirō no hi**	敬老の日	*Respect for the Aged Day*
September 23	**shūbun no hi**	秋分の日	*Autumn Equinox Day*
October 10	**taiiku no hi**	体育の日	*Health-Sports Day*
November 3	**bunka no hi**	文化の日	*Culture Day*
November 23	**kinrō kansha no hi**	勤労感謝の日	*Labor Thanksgiving Day*
December 23	**tennō tanjobi**	天皇誕生日	*Emperor's Birthday*

4.16 Words and Expressions

ACCOMMODATION

shukuhaku	宿泊	*accommodation*
hoteru	ホテル	*Western-style hotel*
ryokan	旅館	*Japanese inn*
minshuku	民宿	*family-run guesthouse*
penshon	ペンション	*Western-style guesthouse*
bijinesu hoteru	ビジネス・ホテル	*no-frills hotel*
shukubō	宿坊	*temple offering accommodations*
yūsu hosuteru	ユース・ホステル	*youth hostel*
kyanpu-jō	キャンプ場	*campsite*
ippaku	一泊	*one-night stay*
washitsu	和室	*Japanese-style room (with futon)*
yōshitsu	洋室	*Western-style room (with bed)*
chōshoku	朝食	*breakfast*
ohiru /chūshoku	お昼・昼食	*lunch*
yūshoku	夕食	*dinner*
daiyokujō	大浴場	*main communal bath*

TRAVELING BY TRAIN

densha	電車	*electric train*
ressha	列車	*train, often refers to a scheduled train*
shinkansen	新幹線	*bullet train*
jiyūseki	自由席	*unreserved seat*
shiteiseki	指定席	*reserved seat*
seisanki	精算機	*fare-adjustment machine*
eki no deguchi	駅の出口	*station exit*
Midori no Madoguchi	みどりの窓口	*Japan Railways reservation office*
jikokuhyō	時刻表	*timetable*
ekiben	駅弁	*station box lunch*

TRAVELING BY CAR

kōsoku dōro	高速道路	*expressway*
ryōkinjo	料金所	*toll gate*
rasshu	ラッシュ	*rush hour*
jūtai	渋滞	*congestion, traffic jam*
sābisu eria	サービス・エリア	*rest area*
pākingu eria	パーキング・エリア	*rest area with limited facilities*
dōro chizu	道路地図	*road map*
rentakā	レンタカー	*car rental*

GENERAL

kankō annai	観光案内	*tourist information*
sakura zensen	桜前線	*the cherry blossom front*

Chapter 5 Shopping

Shopping

I f you're lucky, you might still find in your neighborhood the kind of shop where the owner greets everyone with a loud and hearty **Irasshai** (Welcome!) and sends his regular customers off with an equally spirited **Maido arigatō gozaimasu!** (Thank you for patronizing the shop). But these neighborhood stores are now few and far between.

You don't need to converse much to go shopping these days, so this chapter includes sections on how to deal with automated gas pumps and introduces the basic terms for internet shopping. A dialogue at the pharmacy introduces some medical vocabulary. The rest of the chapter aims to show you what's available, how to master the basics of everyday shopping, and how to explain when things go wrong.

Not that shopping poses a problem in Japan. You'll be spoiled for choice: upmarket department stores, supermarkets, outlet malls, discount stores, huge electrical appliance stores and, of course, the **konbini**.

There are more than 40,000 convenience stores in Japan, far more than the number of neighborhood police boxes or post offices, and the range of services they offer increases year by year. In addition to buying basic foodstuffs and daily necessities, you can pay your bills, post letters, use the ATM for your banking, buy concert tickets, as well as make copies and print out photos. Not only can you send parcels but you can have your local **konbini** receive your parcels (your internet shopping, for example) ready for you to pick up and pay for. Convenience stores also offer that most important facility, a toilet.

But when you feel like a treat, spend a few hours in one of Japan's department stores. Though no longer the central retail institutions they once were, they offer impeccable service and you can easily spend several hours admiring the merchandise, perhaps visiting an art exhibition, and sampling the hustle, bustle and culinary delights of the basement food halls.

Japan has had deflation for decades since the bubble burst in the early 1990s and prices are not high. Bargaining is not practiced except perhaps in flea markets and second-hand stores but competition in most industries is intense and you should shop around when making a big purchase as large electronics and camera stores do give good discounts.

Shops and department stores open at around 10:00 a.m. but the time they close varies, any time between 7:00 p.m. and 9:00 p.m. or later. Convenience stores are often open twenty-four hours. Big shops are open for business on Sundays, although you may find that your local neighborhood greengrocer closes on Sunday for a well-earned rest.

5.01 At a Convenience Store

Kim Young Hee pays a bill and buys some riceballs for lunch. The shop assistant offers to heat them up.

SHOP ASSISTANT:

Irasshaimase. Konnichi wa. Gosen gohyaku gojū en ni nari-masu.

いらっしゃいませ。こんにちは。5,550円になります。

Welcome! Hello. That will be 5,550 yen.

KIM:

Hai.

はい。

Here you are (handing over the money).

SHOP ASSISTANT:

Ichiman-en, o-azukari itashimasu. Pointo cādo, o-mochi de-shō ka.

10,000円、お預かりします。ポイントカード、お持ちでしょうか。

Ten thousand yen. Thank you. Do you have a point card?

KIM:

Iie.

いいえ。

No, I don't.

SHOP ASSISTANT:

Okii hō kara, ichi, ni, san, yon sen en to yonhyaku gojū en no o-kaeshi desu. Hai, ryōkin no hikae desu. O-nigiri at'tamemasu ka?

大きい方から、一、二、三、四千円と450円のお返しになります。はい、料金の控えです。おにぎり、温めますか。

Large amounts first, (counting the notes) that's one, two, three, four thousand yen and 450 yen change. Here's your receipt for the bill. Do you want the riceballs heated up?

KIM:

O-negai shimasu.
お願いします。
Yes, please.

SHOP ASSISTANT:

Mai-baggu, o-mochi deshō ka?
マイバッグお持ちでしょうか。
Do you have your own bag?

KIM:

Hai, arimasu. Arigatō gozaimashita.
はい、あります。　ありがとうございました。
Yes, I do. Thanks.

 ## 5.02   At the Pharmacy

Max goes to a pharmacy to get something for his headache. At the same time he asks about doctors in the area. In Japan you have to do a mini-diagnosis on yourself before choosing which doctor to see. The pharmacist tells him he needs a specialist in internal medicine.

MAX:

Sumimasen. Atama ga itakute, yoku kiku kusuri kudasai.
すみません。頭が痛くて、よく効く薬ください。
Excuse me. I've got a headache. Please give me some good medicine.

PHARMACIST:

Do iu fū na itami desu ka? Kirikiri to itamimasu ka? Shiku shiku to nibui itami desu ka? Soretomo zuki zuki to itamimasu ka?

どういう風な痛みですか。きりきりと痛みますか？しくしくと鈍い痛みですか？それともずきずきと痛みますか。

What kind of pain? Is it a sharp pain? A dull pain? Or a throbbing pain?

MAX:

Gyū to shimetsukeru yō na itami desu yo. Atama mo, kubi mo, kata mo.

ギューッとしめつけるような痛みですよ。頭も、首も、肩も。

It's a heavy, dull, pressing ache. In my head, my neck and my shoulders.

PHARMACIST:

Kinchōtsū desu ne. Kono kusuri ga ii deshō. Yoku kiku shi, i ni mo yasashii desu. Shokugo, ni-jō nonde kudasai. Ashita made naoranakereba, isha ni mite moratte kudasai.

緊張痛ですね。この薬がいいでしょう。よく効くし、胃にもやさしいです。食後、2錠飲んでください。明日まで直らなければ、医者に見てもらってください。

It's a tension-related headache. This medicine is good. It's effective and easy on the stomach. Take two tablets after meals. If you're not better by tomorrow, go and see a doctor.

MAX:

Arigatō gozaimasu. Tokorode, kono chikaku no isha, wakarimasen.

ありがとうございます。ところで、この近くの医者、分かりません。

Thank you. But, I don't know a doctor in this area.

PHARMACIST:

Naika no sensei nē. Ōdori ni Kikuchi naika ga arimasu. Mata, Nishimachi ni ōkina sōgō byōin ga arimasu ne.

内科の先生ねえ。大通りに菊池内科があります。また、西町に大きな総合病院がありますね。

Let me see, a doctor of internal medicine. On the main street there's the Kikuchi Medical Clinic. And then in Nishimachi there's a big general hospital.

MAX:

Arigatō gozaimasu.
ありがとうございます。
Thank you.

PHARMACIST:

O-daiji ni. Sore kara, o-sake wa nonde ikemasen yo.
お大事に。それから、お酒は飲んでいけませんよ。
Take care. And one more thing, you mustn't drink!

5.03 More Ailments

memai ga suru	めまいがする	*I feel dizzy, faint*
hakike ga suru	吐き気がする	*I feel nauseous*
nodo/mimi/mune/ i ga itai	のど・耳・胸・ 胃が痛い	*my throat/ear/chest/ stomach aches*
kaze	風邪	*common cold*
infuruenza	インフルエンザ	*influenza*
zensoku	ぜんそく	*asthma*
shokuchūdoku	食中毒	*food poisoning*
netchūshō	熱中症	*heatstroke*
seiritsū	生理痛	*period pains*
bōkōen	膀胱炎	*cystitis*
tōnyōbyō	糖尿病	*diabetes*
nenza	ねんざ	*sprain*
kossetsu	骨折	*fracture*

5.04 Going to a Dry Cleaner

Because summers in Japan are hot and humid, clothes left in the closet may develop mildew. Most Japanese pack away off-season clothes with mothballs (**bōchū-zai** 防虫剤) in airtight boxes or drawers, a practice known as **koromo-gae** (衣替え, changing clothes over for the season). Despite these precautions, you may end up having to take some of your clothes to the dry cleaner.

DRY CLEANER:

> **Konnichi wa. Ii aki-bare desu ne.**
> こんにちは。いい秋晴れですね。
> *Hello. Beautiful autumn weather, isn't it?*

KATE:

> **Sō desu ne. Demo natsu wa shikke ga ōkute. Mite, kono sētā. Natsu-jū hikidashi ni shimatte oitara, kabi-darake ni natchatta. Kirei ni narimasu ka?**
> そうですね。でも夏は湿気が多くて。見て、このセーター。夏中引き出しにしまっておいたら、カビだらけになっちゃった。きれいににになりますか。
> *Yes, it is. But it was so humid this summer. Look at these sweaters. I left them in the drawer all summer, and now they're covered with mildew. Will they come clean?*

DRY CLEANER:

> **Yatte minai to wakaranai kedo, tabun daijōbu deshō.**
> やってみないと分からないけど、たぶん大丈夫でしょう。
> *I can't say until we've tried, but they'll probably be OK.*

KATE:

> **Ikura kakarimsu ka?**
> いくらかかりますか。
> *How much will it cost?*

DRY CLEANER:

Futsū wa ichi-mai gohyaku-en desu kedo, shimi no guai ni yotte mō sukoshi kakaru ka mo shirenai. Hatsuka ikō nara dekite imasu kara.

普通は一枚500円ですけど、しみの具合によってもう少しかかるかも知れない。20日以降ならできていますから。

Usually it costs 550 yen each, but it depends on the stain. It may cost a little more. They'll be ready after the twentieth.

KATE:

O-negai shimasu.

お願いします。

Thank you.

5.05 Trying on a Garment

Emily is shopping for clothes. But she can't find what she wants.

EMILY:

Kore o shichaku shite ii desu ka?

これを試着していいですか。

May I try this on?

SALESPERSON:

Dōzo, kochira e. Ikaga desu ka?

どうぞ、こちらへ。いかがですか。

Certainly. This way, please. How do you like it?

EMILY:

Omotta hodo yoku nai desu ne. Mō sukoshi mite mimasu. Sumimasen deshita.

思ったほどよくないですね。もう少しみてみます。すみませんでした。

It's not as good as I hoped. I'm going to look around a bit more. Sorry to have troubled you.

SALESPERSON:

Mata, o-koshi kudasai. O-machi shite orimasu.

また、お越しください。お待ちしております。

Please come again. We'll be waiting.

5.06 Shopping for Shoes

Although Japanese stores often have very stylish shoes on display, you might discover that most of them are too small. But things are changing and with a bit of luck, you might find some that fit. By the way, remember that the verb for wearing anything below the waist (shoes, socks, trousers) is **haku** (履く).

EMILY:

Ano kutsu, nijū-yon ten go, arimasu ka?

あの靴、24.5、ありますか。

Those shoes over there, do you have them in size 24.5?

ASSISTANT:

Shōshō o-machi kudasai. Dōzo, o-haki ni natte kudasai.

少々お待ちください。どうぞ、お履きになってください。

One moment, please. Here we are. Please try them on.

CUSTOMER:

Kitsukute hakinikui desu ne. Ue no saizu, arimasen ka?
きつくて履きにくいですね。上のサイズありませんか。
They're tight and don't feel good. Do you have the next size up?

ASSISTANT:

Nijū-yon ten-go made nan' desu yo. Kore wa ikaga desu ka?
24.5までなんですよ。これはいかがですか。
They only go up to 24.5. How about these?

CUSTOMER:

Kore wa hakiyasui desu ne. Kore ni shimasu.
これは履きやすいですね。これにします。
These are comfortable. I'll take these.

5.07   Discount Terms

A sale is usually **sēru** (セール) or **bāgen** (バーゲン). Price reductions are expressed either as a percentage or in units of ten percent, **wari**. So, 10パーセント引き (**juppāsento-biki**) is ten percent off, as is 1割び き (**ichiwari-biki**). 3割引 (**sanwari-biki**) is thirty percent off.
    You may also come across these phrases:

- **O-kaidoku desu yo**
  お買い得ですよ。
  It's a bargain.

- **Yasuku natte orimasu**
  安くなっております。
  It's reduced.

- **Hangaku desu**
  半額です。
  It's half price.

Internet Shopping

Many sites have an English version and there are also search engines in English, but for those of you who want to try shopping on Japanese only websites here's a guide to the language used. These sites are based on the premise that you have a delivery address in Japan and a local method of payment. If you know your way around sites in English a lot of it will be second nature, but there are some pitfalls. For instance, you need to be careful when you input the letters in Japanese. There's a choice of **hiragana** and **katakana** in two sizes, plus the alphabet, so you may get error messages because you input the data in the wrong format.

Here are the basic terms for the buttons. You may be familiar with them already.

検索 **kensaku** *search*

戻る **modoru** *back*   次へ **tsugi e** *next*

続行 **zokkō** *continue*   キャンセル **kyanseru** *cancel*

削除 **sakujo** *delete*

Depending on the site, you may start off with a screen like this to browse:

［商品洋細］
shōhin yōsai *product details*

お茶
o-cha
tea

価格　¥630（税込み）
kakaku (zeikomi) *price (tax included)*

数量：　1　▼
sūryō *quantity*

かごに入れる
kago ni ireru *put in shopping cart*

If it's a bigger site and you're a new customer you'll need to register. The word for registration is 登録 (**tōroku**) so look for phrases like this:

◎ ID登録していない方はこちら(はじめての方)
ID tōroku shite inai kata wa kochira (hajimete no kata)
This (button) for those who are not registered (first time visitors)

You'll be asked to agree to the terms and conditions:

◎ 同意しない
dōi shinai
I do not consent

◎ 同意する
dōi suru
I consent

Then you'll be able to browse as above. On the confirmation screen you can check the contents of your cart and change if necessary:

戻る modoru back		精算 seisan proceed to checkout (lit. payment)		
品名 **Hinmei** *Item*	税込み単価 **zeikomi tanka** *Price per item (tax included)*	数量 **sūryō** *quantity* 変更 **henkō** *change*	小計 **shōkei** *sub-total* 削除 **sakujo** *delete*	
緑茶 **rokucha** *green tea 100g*	630円	1	630円	X
番茶 **bancha** *bancha tea 200g*	350円	1	350円	
合計 **gōkei** *total*			980円	

Now for the difficult part—the customer information screen where you need to input your contact details, delivery address and so on. As stated earlier, you must be very careful how you type in the details. The choices are as follows and you'll see directions on screen:

zenkaku	全角	*full size hiragana or kanji (for your name)*
zenkaku katakana	全角カタカナ	*full size katakana (for your name)*
hankaku sūji	半角数字	*half size numbers (for phone numbers etc)*
hankaku eisūji	半角英数字	*half size numbers and alphabet (for e-mail address and passwords)*

You'll also need to give details of how you intend to pay, usually credit card, cash on delivery (**daikin hikikae** 代金引換), or bank or post office payment.

お客様の情報を入力してください　（*は必須項目です）
o-kyakusama no jōhō o nyūroku shite kudasai (*wa hisshu kōmoku desu)
*please input customer informaton (*required items)*

郵便番号 *　[　　　　] （半角数字、ハイフンなしの7桁）
yubin bangō　　　　　　　　　　　**(hankaku sūji, haifun nashi no nanaketa)**
zip code　　　　　　　　　　　　　*(half size numerals, no hyphen, seven digits)*

住所 *　[　　　　] [選択]
jūsho　　　　　　　　　　**sentaku**
address　　　　　　　　　*select*

続きの住所 *　[　　　　] （全角）マンション名などをご記入ください
tsuzuki no jūsho　　　　　　　　　　**(zenkaku) manshon-mei nado o go-kinyū kudsai**
rest of address　　　　　　　　　*(full size) fill in the name of the apartment etc*

ユーザーID *　[　　　　] （半角英数字　4～24桁）
yūzā ID　　　　　　　　　　**(hankaku eisūji 4 - 24 keta)**
User ID　　　　　　　　　*(half size alphabet and numerals 4 - 24 digits)*

パスワード *　[　　　　] （半角英数字　4～24桁）
pasuwādo　　　　　　　　　　**(hankaku eisūji 4 - 24 keta)**
password　　　　　　　　　*(half size alphabet and numerals 4 - 24 digits)*

パスワード（確認用）*　[　　　　]
pasuwādo(kakuninyō)
password (confirm)

お名前 *　姓 [　　　] 名 [　　　] （全角）
o-namae　**sei**　　　　　**mei**　　　　　**(zenkaku)**
name　　*surname*　　*first name*　　*(full size characters)*

お名前ふりがな *　セイ [　　　] メイ [　　　] （全角カタカナ）
o-namae furigana　　　　　　　　　　**(zenkaku katakana)**
kana for name　　　　　　　　　*(full size katakana)*

電話番号 *　[　] – [　] – [　] （半角数字）
denwa bangō　　　　　　　　　　**(hankaku sūji)**
telephone number　　　　　　　　　*(half size numerals)*

携帯電話番号　[　] – [　] – [　] （半角数字）
keitai denwa bangō　　　　　　　　　　**(hankaku sūji)**
cell phone number　　　　　　　　　*(half size numerals)*

メールアドレス *　[　　　　] （半角英数字）
mēru adoresu　　　　　　　　　　**(hankaku eisūji)**
e-mail address　　　　　　　　　*(half size alphabet and numerals)*

メールアドレス（再入力）*　[　　　　] （半角英数字）
mēru adoresu (sainyūroku)　　　　　　　　　　**(hankaku eisūji)**
e-mail address (input again)　　　　　　　　　*(half size alphabet and numerals)*

性別　○ 男　○ 女
seibetsu　**otoko**　**onna**
sex　　*male*　　*female*

生年月日 *　[---- ▼] [-- ▼] [-- ▼]
seinengappi　　年　　　　月　　　　日
date of birth　　**nen**　　**getsu**　　**hi**
　　　　　　　year　　*month*　　*day*

Finally, choose the date and time you want your shopping delivered, check all the details, press the confirm button and you're done.

お届け先　**o-todoke saki**　*delivery address*

お名前 **o-namae** *name*	
郵便番号 **yūbin bangō** *zip code*	
ご住所 **go-jūsho** *address*	
お電話番号 **o-denwa bangō** *telephone number*	
メールアドレス **mēru adoresu** *e-mail address*	
配達希望日 **haitatsu kibōbi** *requested delivery date*	
配達時間帯 **haitatsu jikantai** *delivery time frame*	

注文確定
chūmon kakutei
confirm order

取り消しはできませんので、ご注意ください
torikeshi wa dekimasen no de, go-chūi kudasai
cannot be cancelled so take care

戻る
modoru
back

5.09 Bargaining

Internet shopping is fine but sometimes it's worth trying to negotiate a reduction in person. Here Lin tries to get a good price at an antiques market.

LIN:

Konnichi wa. Sono kabin wa ikura desu ka?
こんにちは。その花瓶はいくらですか。
Hello. How much is that vase, near you?

ANTIQUE DEALER:

Ichiman-en desu ne.
一万円ですね。
Ten thousand yen.

LIN:

Ichiman!
一万！
Ten thousand!

ANTIQUE DEALER:

Kore wa horidashi-mono desu.
これは掘り出し物です。
It's a good buy.

LIN:

Mō sukoshi yasuku shite moraemasen ka?
もう少し安くしてもらえませんか。
Can you reduce it a little bit?

ANTIQUE DEALER:

Jā, benkyō shite, hassen-en.
じゃ、勉強して、八千円。
OK. I'll knock it down to eight thousand yen.

LIN:

Gosen ni shite yo.
5,000円にしてよ。
Make it five thousand.

ANTIQUE DEALER:

Iya, sore wa muri desu yo.
いや、それは無理ですよ。
No, that's impossible.

LIN:

Jā, rokusen-en.
じゃ、6,000円。
How about six thousand yen?

ANTIQUE DEALER:

Ii deshō. O-make shimashō.
いいでしょう。おまけしましょう。
All right. It's a deal.

5.10   Getting Gas

A visit to the gas station used to be a pleasure rather than a chore: attendants would appear from nowhere and, with loud shouts of **Irasshaimase!,** they would fill your tank, take your money, and even step into the road to stop the traffic, seeing you off with a low bow. You didn't need to get out of the car; you felt like royalty. Alas, such service is a thing of the past, self-service pumps are now commonplace and you may find you have to contend with a machine.

画面をタッチしてください
Gamen o tatchi shite kudasai
Please touch the screen

現金
genkin
cash

カード
kādo
card

ご利用コースを選択してください
Go-riyō kōsu o sentaku shite kudasai
Choose the course you want to use

レギュラー
regyurā
regular

軽油
keiyu
diesel

給油方法を指定してください
Kyūyu hōhō o shitei shite kudasai
Specify how you want to fill up

10リットル
jū rittoru
10 litres

20リットル
nijū rittoru
20 liters

30リットル
sanjū rittoru
30 liters

満タン
mantan
Full Tank

給油量を指定してください
Kyūyuryō o shitei shite kudasai
Specify the quantity

After making your selection, you will hear the following instructions (or something similar):

- **Seidenki shiito o furete kara, nenryō kyappu o ake, akai iro no nozuru de kyūyu shite kudasai.**
  静電気シートを触れてから、燃料キャップを開け、赤い色のノゾルで給油してください。
  After touching the anti-static sheet, open the fuel cap, and fill up with the red nozzle.

And don't forget to pick up your receipt.

5.11 Returning a Product

Michael's not happy with the vacuum cleaner he bought and wants his money back.

MICHAEL:

Kono sōjiki ga kyōryoku da to osshaimashita ga, chittomo gomi o suikomimasen.

この掃除機が強力だとおっしゃいましたが、ちっともゴミを吸い込みません。

You said this was a powerful vacuum cleaner, but it doesn't suck up dirt at all.

SALESPERSON:

Mōshiwake arimasen. Hoka no mono to torikaemashō ka.

申し訳ありません。他のものと取り替えましょうか。

I do apologise. Shall we exchange it for another one?

MICHAEL:

So desu ne. Chiisakute shizuka na mono ga iin' desu ga.

そうですね。小さくて静かなものがいいんですが。

Yes, please. But one that's small and quiet would be good (is what I'm looking for).

SALESPERSON:

Dōzo. O-tashikame kudasai.

どうぞ。お確かめください。

Here you are. Check them out.

MICHAEL:

Dame desu ne. Yappari, daikin o kaeshite moraimasho.

だめですね。やっぱり、代金を返してもらいましょう。

They're no good. I'll have my money back after all.

SALESPERSON:

Mōshiwake gozaimasen.

申し訳ございません。

I do apologize.

5.12 Complaining About Defects

- **Shimi/kizu ga tsuite imasu.**
  しみ / 傷がついています。
  This is stained/chipped.

- **Hibi ga haitte imasu.**
  ひびが入っています。
  This is cracked.

- **Kono chiizu wa kinō kattan' desu ga, furukute taberaremasen.**
  このチーズは昨日かったんですが、古くてたべられません。
  I bought this cheese yesterday but it's so old that we can't eat it.

- **Kono wain no koruku ga kawaite ite, poro-poro shite nuke-nakattan' desu yo.**
  このワインのコルクが乾いていて、ぽろぽろして抜けなかったんですよ。
  The cork in this wine was so dried up that it crumbled and couldn't be pulled out.

- **Raberu no tōri sentaku shitara, chijinde shimattan' desu.**
  ラベルの通り洗濯したら、縮んでしまったんです。
  It shrank, even though I washed it according to the instructions on the label.

5.13 Describing Breakdowns

When one of the machines in your life breaks down you'll have to describe the symptoms to find out if it can be repaired. The Japanese language is rich in onomatopoeic words to describe sounds; and this section includes some of these. I hope they're useful as well as fun to learn.

PLUMBING:

- **Toire ga tsumatte imasu.**
  トイレが詰まっています。
  The toilet's clogged.

- **Nagashi no mizu ga nagaremasen.**
  流しの水が流れません。
  The sink won't drain.

- **Furo ga kusai.**
  風呂がくさい。
  The bath smells bad.

TELEVISION:

- **Dengen wa hairimasu ga, gamen mo oto mo demasen.**
  電源は入りますが、画面も音もでません。
  It switches on, but there's no picture or sound.

- **Gamen ga masshiro de, eizō ga demasen.**
  画面が真っ白で、映像がでません。
  The screen is white and there's no picture.

- **Gamen ga chira-chira shite, zatsuon ga shimasu.**
  画面がちらちらして、雑音がします。
  The picture jumps and the sound buzzes.

PHONE:

- **Pipipi to iu keikokuon ga natte imasu.**
  ピピピという警告音が鳴っています。
  It's beeping—the alarm's sounding.

- **Deisupurei ga kuraku nari, nanimo hyōji saremasen.**
  ディスプレイが暗くなり、何も表示されません。
  The display's gone dark; nothing is shown.

- **Mēru o jushin dekimasu ga, hasshin wa dekimasen.**
  メールを受信できますが、発信はできません。
  I can receive messages but I can't send any.

APPLIANCES:

- **Suitchi wa hairimasu ga, atatamaranai/hienai/mawaranai/ no desu.**
  スイッチは入りますが、温まらない / 冷えない / 回らないのです。
  It switches on but doesn't heat/cool/go.

- **Taimā/Sāmosutatto ga kowarete imasu.**
  タイマー / サーモスタットがこわれています。
  The timer/thermostat is broken.

- **Sentakki wa dassui no toki ni gata gata to ōki na oto ga narimasu.**
  洗濯機は脱水のときにガタガタと大きな音が鳴ります。
  The washing machine when it spins makes a loud clattering noise.

CARS:

- **Enjin ga kakarimasen.**
  エンジンがかかりません。
  The engine won't start.

- **Enjin ga burun-burun to natte, togireru kanji ga shimasu.**
  エンジンがぶるんぶるんとなって、途切れる感じがします。
  The engine's running unevenly. It feels like it's jerking.

- **Akuseru o fumu to, ushiro kara gishi gishi to oto ga shimasu.**
  アクセルを踏むと、後ろからぎしぎしと音がします。
  When I tread on the accelerator, it makes a creaking noise at the back.

COMPUTER:

- **Passwādo o wasurete shimaimashita.**
  パスワードを忘れてしまいました。
  I've forgotten the password.

- **Dengen o ireru to, erā-messēji ga hyōji sare, OS ga kidō dekimasen.**
  電源を入れると、エラーメッセージが表示され、OSが起動できません。
  When I switch it on, a message is displayed and the OS doesn't start.

- **Hādo deisuku ga kakkon kakkon, kacha kacha to iu oto o shi-mashita.**

 ハードデイスクがカッコンカッコン、カチャカチャという音をしました。

 The hard disc clinked and clattered.

- **Hādo deisuku no naiyō o ayamatte keshite shimaimashita.**

 ハードデイスクの内容を誤って消してしまいました。

 I deleted the contents of the hard disc by mistake.

5.14 Words and Expressions

o-tsukai	お使い	*daily errands*
kaimono	買い物	*shopping (usually in the neighborhood)*
shoppingu	ショッピング	*shopping expedition (usually to a large shopping district)*
mise/shōten	店・商店	*shop*
shōtengai	商店街	*shopping street, arcade*
sūpā	スーパー	*supermarket*
yakkyoku	薬局	*pharmacy*
sakaya	酒屋	*liquor store*
hanaya	花屋	*florist*
kuriininguya	クリーニング屋	*dry cleaner*
depāto	デパート	*department store*
depachika	デパチカ	*basement food hall in a department store*

konbini	コンビニ	*convenience store*
kyaku	客	*customer*
reji	レジ	*cash register*
o-tsuri, o-kaeshi	おつり・お返し	*change*

denshi manē
  o-saifu keitai
	電子マネー
	  おサイフケイタイ
		e-money,
		  cell phone e-money

netto tsūhan	ネット通販	*internet shopping*
koshō (suru)	故障 (する)	*breakdown, to breakdown*
hoshōsho	保証書	*guarantee, warranty*
shūri (suru)	修理 (する)	*repairs*

hokōsha tengoku	歩行者天国	*pedestrians' paradise*
		  (shopping street closed
		  to traffic)

Chapter 6

Banks and Delivery Services

Banks and Delivery Services

Banking within Japan is very efficient. From ATM machines, either at the banks or at the thousands of convenience stores dotted around the country, you can withdraw and deposit cash, make payments, pay bills, set up direct debits, update your passbook and get a new one. The machines even have virtual bank staff, cartoon characters who bow politely to thank you for each transaction.

It's a different story when it comes to international banking. At the time of this writing one hears of much frustration in this area. You may find that ATMs do not accept your overseas credit card, as you would expect when travelling abroad. So before you leave home, find out exactly where you will be able to use your card. As a general rule, stick to the major national banks, and if you're travelling outside the main tourist areas, take cash or have some other backup means of finance. Similarly, overseas remittances and receiving funds from abroad can be time-consuming and expensive. Again, go only to the major national banks or to the post office, which has very reasonable charges.

The Japan Post Bank, or **Yūcho Ginko**, is the financial arm of the Japanese post office and holds the majority of the nation's private savings. It offers a good service for sending and receiving funds from abroad, and it may be worth opening an account not only to avail yourself of this service, but also to have access to ATMs in post offices nationwide.

Japan Post is in charge of traditional mail services. It has a good website in English so this chapter will just introduce a few special services which may be new to you.

Regular mail is fast and reliable but you can pay a small extra fee to have special next-day delivery (**sokutatsu**) which delivers every day of the year, including Sundays and holidays. If you're not at home to sign for registered mail or there's a parcel that doesn't fit in the mailbox, a notice will be left. To have the mail redelivered, phone the call center within two weeks with the relevant details. Or, you can take the notice and some form of ID to the post office and pick it up yourself.

Money orders do exist but you can also send cash by registered mail. It saves the recipient a trip to the bank or post office, and it's used for sending special envelopes of money (see the chapter on Gifts).

The post office offers attractive postcards for sending at New Year's and in midsummer. New Year cards are delivered all together on New Year's Day (more in the last chapter on Letters).

Finally, when you move, the post office will forward your mail free of charge for one year. Pick up a form from the post office or print one out from the website.

Delivery services, which transport all types of parcels, provide an alternative to the postal service. They are prompt, reliable, and very popular. To send a parcel, take it to a nearby **takkyūbin** or **takuhaibin** pick-up point. For heavy items like skis, suitcases, or golf clubs, you can call for them to be picked up from your home. Sending fresh food is no problem, either: choose the "chilled" option and your parcel will be transported by refrigerated truck and stored in refrigerated warehouses. You can choose what time of day to have the item delivered, choose to pay on delivery, and request confirmation that the goods have arrived.

Changing Money

Kim says she wants to change South Korean won to Japanese yen. To use this phrase, be sure to pronounce clearly the "e" in **kaetai** (換えたい I'd like to change). Or you could just put the cash on the counter and say **en o kaitai** (買いたい I'd like to buy yen).

KIM:

Kankoku won o Nihon en ni kaetain' desu ga. Kyō no rēto wa ikura desu ka?

韓国ウォンを日本円に換えたいんですが、今日のレートはいくらですか。

I'd like to change some Korean won into Japanese yen. What's today's rate?

TELLER:

Kankoku won no kai-ne wa zero ten zeronana-en to natte orimasu.

韓国ウォンの買値は0.07円となっております。

We're buying won at 0.07 yen.

KIM:

Mata sagatchatta! Komatta na. Kore dake kaemashō.

また下がっちゃった。困ったな。これだけ換えましょう。

It's down again! Oh, no! I'll just change this much then.

TELLER:

Koko ni sain, o-negai shimasu. Sore kara pasupōto o misete kudasai.

ここにサインお願いします。それからパスポートを見せてください。

Please sign here. And show me your passport, please.

6.02   At the Bank

Bank staff will show you how to use the machines.

- **Sumimasen. ATM no tsukai-kata o oshiete kudasai.**
  すみません。ATMの使い方を教えてください。
  Excuse me. Could you show me how to use the ATM?

- **Genkin o furikomitai desu / Kōza kara furikomitai desu.**
  現金を振り込みたいです/口座から振り込みたいです。
  I'd like to make a payment from cash/from my account.

- **Denwa-dai o jidō furikae ni shitai desu.**
  電話代を自動振り替えにしたいです。
  I'd like the telephone bill deducted automatically from my account.

- **Kichō shitai desu.**
  記帳したいです。
  I want to print the transactions (in my passbook).

6.03   Opening an Account

When you make your first deposit, the bank will show its appreciation by giving you a small gift.

LIN:

Kōza o hirakitain' desu ga.
口座を開きたいんですが。
I'd like to open an account.

TELLER:

Inkan o o-mochi deshō ka?
印鑑をお持ちでしょうか。
Do you have a name stamp?
[note: a name stamp can be used in place of a signature. More about these in the chapter on Officialdom]

LIN:

Motte imasen keredo.
持っていませんけれど。
No, I don't have one.

TELLER:

Ja, sain de kekkō desu no de, go-jūsho to o-namae to kyō ireru kingaku (ikura demo yoroshii desu keredo) o-kaki kudasai. Sore kara honnin kakunin dekiru mono ga hitsuyō desu.
じゃ、サインで結構ですので、ご住所とお名前と今日入れる金額（いくらでもよろしいですけれど）お書きください。それから本人確認できるものが必要です。
Then a signature will do. Please fill in your address, your name, and how much you will deposit today (it doesn't matter how much). And we need some form of ID.

LIN:

Hai.
はい。
All right.

TELLER:

De wa, kochira ni yon keta no anshō bangō o kinyū shite kudasai. Kādo wa isshūkan naishi tōka no uchi ni go-jitaku no hō ni todokimasu.
では、こちらに4ケタの暗証番号を記入してください。カードは一週間ないし10日の内にご自宅に届きます。
And, will you please write a four-digit PIN number here. The card will be delivered to your home within a week or ten days.

LIN:

Yoroshiku o-negai shimasu.
よろしくお願いします。
Thank you.

At the Post Office

Here are some basic phrases for when you go to the post office.

- **Hyaku-en kitte ni-mai kudasai.**
  100円切手2枚ください。
  Two one-hundred-yen stamps, please.

- **Amerika made no e-hagaki wa kōkūbin de ikura desu ka?**
  アメリカまでの絵葉書は航空便でいくらですか。
  How much is it to send a postcard to America by airmail?

- **Kore wa sumōru paketto de ikimasu ka?**
  これはスモールパケットで行きますか。
  Will this go at the small-packet rate?

Mailing Money

You can send cash to addresses in Japan by registered mail. Ask at the post office for the special double envelope, which you seal and re-seal with your initials or a name stamp. You can send up to five hundred thousand yen, and you'll receive full compensation if it goes astray.

EMILY:

Genkin kakitome no fūtō o ichi-mai kudasai. O-iwai o okuri-masu.

現金書留の封筒を1枚ください。お祝いを送ります。

One registered money-mail envelope, please. I'm sending (some money for) a celebration.

CLERK:

Hai. Dōzo.

はい、どうぞ。

OK. Here you are.

EMILY:

Sokutatsu de o-negai shimasu.

速達でお願いします。

By express delivery, please.

CLERK:

Ikura haitte imasu ka?

いくら入っていますか。

How much is in it?

EMILY:

Gosen-en.

5,000円。

¥5,000.

CLERK:

Nanahyaku nanajū-en ni narimasu ne. Dashite okimasu kara.

770円になりますね。出しておきますから。

That'll be ¥770. I'll send it from here.

EMILY:

O-negai shimasu.

お願いします。

Thank you.

6.06　Wiring Money Abroad

Max goes to a post office to see if he can wire money abroad. You can send and receive money between bank accounts or send a money transfer to a certain address. The charge (at the time of writing) is the same for any amount and for all countries.

MAX:

Igirisu no haha ni o-kane o okuritain' desu ga, koko kara dekimasu ka?

イギリスの母にお金を送りたいんですが、ここからできますか。

I want to send money to my mother in the UK. Can I do it from here?

CLERK:

Kokusai sōkin dekimasu yo. Hōhō mittsu arimashite, kōza-kan no sōkin, kōza-ate no sōkin, soshite jūsho-ate no sōkin ga arimasu.

国際送金できますよ。方法三つありまして、口座間の送金、口座あての送金、それから住所あての送金があります。

Yes, you can do an overseas remittance. There are three ways: transfer between accounts, payment to an account and payment to an address.

MAX:

Naruhodo. Yūcho no kōza kara Igirisu no haha no ginkō kōza ni jūman o sōkin shitai desu.

なるほど。ゆうちょの口座からイギリスの母の銀行口座に10万を送金したいです。

I see. I want to send 100,000 from my Post Bank account to my mother's bank account in England.

CLERK:

Sore de wa, yōshi wa kochira ni narimasu.

それでは、用紙はこちらになります。

Well, here's the form.

MAX:

Sumimasen. Chotto oshiete kudasai. Uketorinin to iu no wa mukō no haha no koto desu ka.

すみません。ちょっと教えてください。受取人というのは向こうの母のことですか。

Excuse me. Can you help (lit. teach) me? Does "Payee" mean my mother abroad?

CLERK:

Sō desu ne. Uketorinin wa okāsama desu ne. Okāsama no o-namae to o-tokoro o koko ni kaite kudasai.

そうですね。受取人はお母様ですね。お母様のお名前とおところをここに書いてください。

Yes, The payee would be your mother. Write you mother's name and address here.

MAX:

Hai. Ikura ni narimasu ka?

はい。いくらになりますか。

All right. Here you are. How much will it be?

CLERK:

Tesūryō wa nisen gohyaku-en desu no de, zenbu de jūman nisen gohyaku-en ni narimasu.

手数料は2,500円ですので、全部で102,500円になります。

The charge is ¥2,500 so the total is ¥102,500.

6.07 Delivery Services

An alternative to sending parcels through the post office is to use a private delivery service. Takuya, who's recovered from his illness, wants to do some sightseeing before catching the train back to Tokyo, so he decides to have his luggage delivered to his home.

TAKUYA:

Chotto o-kiki shimasu. Chikaku ni nimotsu o okuru tokoro wa arimasu ka?
ちょっとお聞きします。近くに荷物を送るところはありますか。
Can I ask you something? Is there somewhere nearby where I can send luggage?

HOTEL RECEPTIONIST:

Hai, baiten ni takuhaibin ga gozaimasu.
はい、売店に宅配便がございます。
Yes, there's a delivery service in the hotel shop.

TAKUYA:

Sumimasen. Kono nimotsu o Tōkyō no jitaku e okuritai desu.
すみません。この荷物を東京の自宅へ送りたいです。
Excuse me. I'd like to send this luggage to my home in Tokyo.

HOTEL SHOP ASSISTANT:

Hai. Tōkyō wa nimotsu hitotsu ni tsuki sen-en ni narimasu. Soshite fukuro ga hyaku gojū-en desu ga.
はい。東京は荷物一つにつき1,000円になります。そして袋が150円ですが。
Fine. For Tokyo, it's one thousand yen per bag. The (protective) bags are one hundred and fifty yen each

TO 郵便番号 **yūbinbangō** *zip code*	□□□－□□□□	

お届け先

おところ
o-tokoro
address
_____

おなまえ
o-namae
name
_____

でんわ
denwa
tel.
_____

FROM 郵便番号 **yūbinbangō** *zip code*	□□□ □□□□	

ご依頼主

おところ
o-tokoro
address
_____

おなまえ
o-namae
name   様
_____

でんわ
denwa
tel.
_____

配達希望日 **haitatsu kibōbi** *desired delivery date*	
月 **tsuki** *month*	日 **hi** *day*

配達希望時間帯 **haitatsu kibō jikantai** *desired delivery time*		
午前中 **gozenchū** *morning*		午後 **gogo** *afternoon*
夕方 **yūgata** *evening*	夜間 **yakan** *night*	希望 なし **kibō nashi** *no preference*

品名 **hinmei** *item*

TAKUYA:

Sore ja, hitotsu ni matomete ii desu ka?
それじゃ、一つにまとめていいですか。
Then may I put everything in one bag?

HOTEL SHOP ASSISTANT:

Hai, hitotsu ni dekimasu. Ashita todokimasu ga, shitei jikan wa nanji goro shimasu ka.
はい、一つにできます。明日届きますが、指定時間は何時ごろしますか。
Yes, you can [put into one]. It will be delivered tomorrow. What time of day do you want it delivered?

TAKUYA:

Kaeranai uchi ni todoku to ikenai no de, yūgata, o-negai shimasu.

帰らないうちに届くといけないので、夕方、お願いします。

It mustn't arrive before I get home, so in the evening please.

HOTEL SHOP ASSISTANT:

Sore de wa, yūgata shichi-ji to ku-ji no aida.

それでは、夕方7時と9時の間。

So, (it will be delivered) between 7 and 9 p.m.

TAKUYA:

Hai. Yoroshiku o-negai shimasu.

はい。よろしくお願いします。

Fine. Thank you.

6.08 Words and Expressions

FOREIGN EXCHANGE

gaika ryōgae	外貨両替	*foreign exchange*
kawase rēto	為替レート	*exchange rate*
tsūka	通貨	*currency*
tesūryō	手数料	*commission, handling fee*
en ni kansan suru	円に換算する	*to convert into yen*

POST OFFICE

yūbinkyoku	郵便局	*post office*
posuto	ポスト	*mailbox*
kitte	切手	*stamp*
tegami	手紙	*letter*

kansei hagaki	官製はがき	*prestamped postcard*
nengajō	年賀状	*New Year postcard*
kozutsumi	小包	*parcel; small package*
sumōru paketto / kogata hōsōbutsu	スモールパケット・小型包装物	*small package*
kōkūbin	航空便	*airmail*
kakitome	書留	*registered mail*
sokutatsu	速達	*express mail*
tenkyo todoke	転居届け	*change-of-address*
Kurisumasu mēru no sashi-dashi kigen	クリスマスメールの差出期限	*last mailing date for Christmas*

BANK

ginkō	銀行	*bank*
yokin/ yokin suru	預金・預金する	*deposit/ to make a deposit*
hikidashi	引き出し	*withdrawal*
genkin o orosu	現金を下ろす	*to take cash out of the bank*
futsū kōza	普通口座	*current account*
teiki yokin	定期預金	*time deposit*
yokin tsūchō	預金通帳	*bankbook, passbook*
sōkin/furikomi	送金・振込み	*remittance, bank transfer*
jidō furikomi	自動振込み	*direct debit*
yūshi/rōn	融資・ローン	*loan*
rishi	利子	*interest*
furikome sagi	振込め詐欺	*A fraud committed by swindlers who telephone victims (especially the elderly) and trick them into sending money through ATMs*

Chapter 7 Business

Business

As in any country, communication is the key to good relationships with people both inside and outside the company. The Japanese work hard at this, and business people from overseas will have to work even harder to break down barriers and establish good working relationships. In business hours there will be meetings and visits to clients; ourside of business hours, time spent with colleagues and clients will give you an insight into what is really happening. And playing golf, although not the national obsession it once was, will give you more opportunities to build up relationships with business acquaintances.

The language used in business is probably the most formal you will come across and there are rules of etiquette that you need to get used to. The presentation of business cards is a ceremony in itself. But don't be put off. It might help to remember that many Japanese are probably just as ill at ease as you are—so try to be relaxed. It is important to get the formalities right, but it's equally important to get to true communication as soon as you can. Be friendly and open, know your subject and you'll be fine.

Let us suppose you are about to go to your first formal business engagement in Japan and you want to know how to prepare for it. For one thing, make sure you have business cards showing your company or affiliation. Have a few general comments ready in Japanese, perhaps concerning the weather or a recent news event. Also be sure to dress neatly; this depends on the industry and attitudes are changing but, generally, it means suit and tie for men, and jacket for women. Japanese are sticklers for punctuality so give yourself ample time to find your destination.

The card-exchanging ceremony takes place after you are shown into the meeting room (incidentally, there are even rules about where to sit: visitors sit on the chairs opposite the door; and the top seat is the seat furthest from the door). In this ceremony everyone stands to one side of the tables. When offering your card, present it so that your name is right side up as it faces the recipient. At the same time, bow and say your name. You're supposed to receive the other person's card with both hands, but it's difficult when you're trying to juggle your card case as well. Use the case to receive the card. Look first at the title, to see what level of person you are dealing with, then look at the name. You can say the name out loud (it will help you remember it). Take your seat, putting the cards in front of you on the table. If you don't know the reading of someone's name it's a good opening gambit to ask. People are generally more than happy to explain the background to an unusual name and it's a good ice-breaker.

Don't be in too much of a hurry to get to business. First, people have to register that you can function in the language; next, you have to draw them in. Try to blend, try to find points of similarity. People will be pleased if you show you have noticed something about their country and praise it. Food and drink are "safe" topics.

During the conversation, generally address people by their titles without the name, for example, **kachō**, **manejā**. If the person doesn't have a title, use –**san** after their name. Don't use all three, **Kobabyashi buchō-san** is incorrect.

Others may use formal language throughout the meeting, but no one will think the worse of you if you slip into neutral language (using the –**masu** form of verbs) after the initial civilities are through. At the end of the meeting, you'll find speech becoming formal again, so you will leave a good final impression if you use the polite set expressions to thank your hosts for their time and to say goodbye.

The conversations in this chapter deal with the courtesy call (**aisatsu**), a short visit to a client, customer or anyone else connected with the business. Courtesy calls are made during the year, especially when people change positions or companies, or when new business deals have been settled. During the last weeks in December and again in the first weeks of January, people make calls to thank others for their custom during the past year and to express the hope that the relationship will continue through the coming year.

7.01 Visiting a Client's Office

When you visit someone on business in Japan, you should arrive several minutes early and make yourself known at reception.

> MICHAEL:
>
> **Ekoshisutemu no Tērā to mōshimasu ga, kōbai no Takahashi-san, o-negai shimasu. Niji ni o-yakusoku o itadaite orimasu.**
> エコシステムのテーラーと申しますが、購買の高橋さんお願いします。2時にお約束をいただいております。
> *My name is Taylor and I'm from EcoSystems. I would like (to meet with) Mr. Takahashi from the purchasing department. I have (received) an appointment at 2 p.m.*
>
> VOICE:
>
> **Shōshō o-machi kudasai.**
> 少々お待ちください。
> *One moment please.*

TAKAHASHI:

Tērā-san desu ka? O-machi shite orimashita. Takahashi desu.

テーラーさんですか。お待ちしておりました。高橋です。

Mr. Mitchell? I've been expecting you. I'm Takahashi.

MICHAEL:

Hajimemashite. Tērā desu. Kyō wa o-isogashii tokoro, arigatō gozaimasu.

はじめまして。テーラーです。きょうはお忙しいところ、ありがとうございます。

How do you do? My name is Taylor. Thank you for making time to see me today.

TAKAHASHI:

Tondemo nai desu yo. Kochira e dōzo.

とんでもないですよ。どうぞこちらへ。

Not at all. Please come this way.

7.02   Introducing People

Takahashi decides to introduce Michael and his colleagues to the CEO of the company.

MICHAEL (presenting his card) :

Ecoshisutemu no Tērā de gozaimasu.

エコシステムのテーラーでございます。

My name is Taylor and I'm from EcoSystems.

CEO:

Hajimemashite. Hashimoto de gozaimasu.

はじめまして。橋本でございます。

How do you do? My name is Hashimoto.

MICHAEL:

Hajimemashite. Dōzo yoroshiku o-negai itashimasu.
Go-shōkai shimasu. Eigyō no Satō de gozaimasu. Denki ji-
dōsha no supesharisuto de gozaimasu.
はじめまして。どうぞよろしくお願いいたします。
ご紹介します。営業の佐藤でございます。電気自動車のス
ペシャリストでございます。
I'm very pleased to meet you. Let me introduce you. This is Sato,
from sales. She's a specialist in electric vehicles.

SATO:

Hajimemashite. Yoroshiku o-negai itashimasu.
はじめまして。よろしくお願いいたします。
Glad to meet you.

CEO:

Ima tantō no mono mo yobimasu no de, dōzo, o-kake kudasai.
今、担当の者も呼びますので、どうぞ、お掛けください。
I'll just call in the person who is working on this project so please
sit down.

7.03 Meeting with a Client

As in most other countries in the world, a meeting will often begin with
polite small talk before proceeding to the business in hand.

MICHAEL:

Mae ni Rarii kenkyūjo ni imashita ga, shachō wa Nōsu Karo-
raina go-zonji desu ka?
前にラリー研究所にいましたが、社長はノースカロライナ
ーご存知ですか。

I used to be with our research institute in Raleigh. Are you familiar with North Carolina?

HASHIMOTO:

Ē. Kengaku shita koto ga arimasu yo.
えー。見学したことがありますよ。
Yes. I've visited it.

MICHAEL:

Iya, hontō desu ka? Itsu-goro irasshitan' desu ka?
いや、本当ですか。いつごろいらっしたんですか。
Really? When did you go?

HASHIMOTO:

Dōji tahatsu tero jiken no chokugo deshita yo. Hikōki ga amari nakattan' desu ga, dōshitemo ikitakute.
同時多発テロ事件の直後でしたよ。飛行機があまりなかったんですが、どうしても行きたくて。
It was right after 9–11. There weren't many planes flying but I was really intent on going.

MICHAEL:

Sasuga desu ne. Onsha ga chōdo shin-enerugii ni chikara o ire-dashita koro desu ne. Sono go wa ichijirushii hatten desu ne.
さすがですね。御社がちょうど新エネルギーに力を入れだしたころですね。その後は著しい発展ですね。
That's amazing. That was about the time your company started concentrating on new forms of energy. Since then, things have really come a long way.

HASHIMOTO:

Ossharu tōri desu. Hanashi ga kawarimasu ga, kyō wa nani-ka?
おっしゃるとおりです。話が変わりますが、今日は何か。
Yes, indeed [lit. as you say]. However [lit. to change the subject], what can I do for you today?

MICHAEL:

Jitsu wa, atarashii seihin no go-shōkai ni agarimashita.
実は、新しい製品のご紹介に上がりました。
Well, I've come to tell you about our new product.

7.04 Starting a Conversation

These general remarks can be used to start a conversation.

- **Mezurashii myōji desu ne. Dochira no go-shusshin desu ka?**
  珍しい名字ですね。どちらのご出身ですか。
  That's an unusual surname. Where are you from?

- **Atsui hi ga tsuzukimasu ne. Shigoto e no eikyō wa?**
  暑い日が続きますね。仕事への影響は？
  This hot weather doesn't let up, does it? Does it affect your business?

- **Onsha no shinseihin o sassoku kaimashita. Sugoi desu ne.**
  御社の新製品を早速買いました。すごいですね。
  I immediately bought your company's new product. It's really good.

- **Senjitsu shinbun de haiken shimashita ga, onsha ga kondo Betonamu de kōjō o shinsetsu suru yō desu ne. Masu-masu o-sakan desu ne.**
  先日、新聞で拝見しましたが、御社が今度ヴェトナムで工場を新設するようですね。ますますお盛んですね。
  I saw in the newspaper that your company is going to build a new plant in Vietnam. Your company's doing very well, isn't it?

Below are comments that will direct the conversation toward the business in hand.

- **Bijinesu wa ikaga desu ka?**
  ビジネスはいかがですか。
  How's business?

- **Gyōkai no keiki wa ikaga desu ka?**
  業界の景気はいかがですか。
  What's the situation like in your industry?

- **Urete imasu ka?**
  売れていますか。
  How are sales?

- **Gen'yu kakaku ga neage saresō desu ga, eikyō wa dō desu ka?**
  原油価格が値上げされそうですが、影響はどうですか。
  It looks as if the price of oil will be raised. How will that affect you?

- **Kyō mo mata en-daka/en-yasu ni ugokimashita ne.**
  今日もまた円高・円安に動きましたね。
  The yen's stronger/weaker again today.

7.05 Year-end Courtesy Call (1)

During December, sales staff and management make year-end calls to thank clients for their business during the year. This dialogue gives examples of the typical expressions that are exchanged during such a visit. The visit also gives Michael a chance to find out what's happened to his proposal.

MICHAEL:

Kotoshi wa iro-iro to o-sewa ni narimashita. Arigatō gozaima-shita. Rainen mo yoroshiku o-negai itashimasu.

今年はいろいろとお世話になりました。ありがとうございました。来年もよろしくお願いいたします。

Thank you for all your help this year. We look forward to working with you next year as well.

TAKAHASHI:

Sore wa dōmo waza-waza arigatō gozaimasu. Kochira koso iro-iro to o-sewa ni narimashita.

それはどうもわざわざありがとうございます。こちらこそいろいろとお世話になりました。

Thank you for taking the trouble to visit us. We are the ones who should be thanking you for your help.

MICHAEL:

Tokorode, senjitsu no ken nan desu ga, shinchoku jōkyō wa?

ところで、先日の件なんですが、進捗状況は?

By the way, about the matter [we discussed] the other day. Any progress?

TAKAHASHI:

Junchō ni susunde imasu yo. Rainen sōsō, gutaiteki na hanashi ga dekiru to omoimasu yo.

順調に進んでいますよ。来年早々、具体的な話ができると思いますよ。

It's proceeding satisfactorily. Early in the new year I think we'll be able to have some concrete discussions.

MICHAEL:

Yokatta desu ne. Sore de wa, rainen mo yoroshiku o-negai itashimasu. Mina-san, yoi o-toshi o o-mukae kudasai.

よかったですね。それでは、来年もよろしくお願いいたします。皆さんよいお年をお迎えください。

Great. We look forward to continuing our relationship with you next year. Happy New Year to all of you.

TAKAHASHI:

Waza-waza go-teinei ni arigatō gozaimashita. Dōzo, yoi o-toshi o.

わざわざご丁寧にありがとうございました。どうぞ、よいお年を。

Thank you for visiting. Have a happy New Year.

7.06 Year-end Courtesy Call (2)

Year-end courtesy calls, which can be made without an appointment, provide excellent opportunities for meeting people. The only difficulty may be that the people you go to see are out doing their rounds! If this happens, leave your card and proceed to your next destination.

MICHAEL:

Ekoshisutemu no Tērā desu ga nenmatsu no go-aisatsu ni ukagaimashita. Kobayashi-jōmu wa irasshaimasu deshō ka?

エコシステムのテーラーですが年末のご挨拶に伺いました。小林常務はいらっしゃいますでしょうか。

I'm Taylor from EcoSystems. I've come to make a year-end call. Is Mr. Kobayashi in?

MEMBER OF STAFF:

Ainiku Kobayashi wa ima gaishutsu-chū desu.
あいにく、小林は今、外出中です。
I'm afraid he's out right now.

MICHAEL:

**Sore de wa, meishi o buchō ni o-watashi itadakemasu ka?
Kotoshi wa iro-iro to o-sewa ni narimashita. Ecoshisutemu no
Tērā ga nenmatsu no go-aisatsu ni ukagaimashita to tsutaete
kudasai.**
それでは、名詞を部長にお渡しいただけますか。今年はい
ろいろとお世話になりました。エコシステムのテーラーが
年末のご挨拶に伺いましたと伝えてください。
*Then would you give him my card? I wanted to thank him for all
his help this year. Please tell him that Taylor from EcoSystems
came to see him.*

MEMBER OF STAFF:

Kashikomarimashita. Waza-waza arigatō gozaimashita.
かしこまりました。わざわざありがとうございました。
Certainly. Thank you for calling.

7.07 New Year Courtesy Call

New Year courtesy calls should be made within the first two weeks
after returning to work.

MICHAEL:

**Akemashite omedetō gozaimasu. Kyūnen-chū wa iro-iro to
o-sewa ni narimashite, arigatō gozaimashita. Honnen mo
yoroshiku o-negai itashimasu.**

あけましておめでとうございます。旧年中はいろいろとお世話になりまして、ありがとうございました。本年もよろしくお願いいたします。

Happy New Year. We would like to thank you for all your help last year. We look forward to working with you this year as well.

KOBAYASHI:

Omedetō gozaimasu. Kochira koso honnen mo yoroshiku o-negai itashimasu.

おめでとうございます。こちらこそ本年もよろしくお願いいたします。

Happy New Year. We too look forward to the relationship continuing through this year.

MICHAEL:

Jōmu no o-shōgatsu wa ikaga deshita ka? Eigo wa o-tassha de irasshaimasu no de, hyotto shitara, kaigai ryokō de mo saremashita ka?

常務のお正月はいかがでしたか。英語はお達者でいらっしゃいますので、ひょっとしたら、海外旅行でもされましたか。

Director, how was your New Year? Your English is good, perhaps you went abroad?

KOBAYASHI:

Iya, zenzen. Doko e mo dekakenakatta desu yo.

いや、ぜんぜん。どこへも出かけなかったですよ。

No, not at all. We didn't go anywhere.

MICHAEL:

Sore wa sore wa. Tokoro de, kotoshi no keiki wa dō deshō ne?

それはそれは。ところで今年の景気はどうでしょうね。

I see. By the way, I wonder what kind of year it will be?

KOBAYASHI:

Ii toshi de atte hoshii mono desu ne.

いい年であってほしいものですね。

I hope it's a good year.

MICHAEL:

Watakushidomo to no tori-hiki ga fueru to iin' desu ga ne.

私どもとの取引が増えるといいんですがね。

I hope that this year your company will continue doing more and more business with us.

KOBAYASHI:

Mochiron sō negaitai desu yo.

もちろんそう願いたいですよ。

Of course, we hope so too.

MICHAEL:

Sore-dewa, o-isogashii tokoro o arigatō gozaimashita.

それでは、お忙しいところをありがとうございました。

Thank you for giving up your time to see me today.

KOBAYASHI:

Iie. Waza-waza arigatō gozaimashita.

いいえ。わざわざありがとうございました。

Not at all. Thank you for coming.

MICHAEL:

Sore-dewa, kore de shitsurei shimasu.

それでは、これで失礼します。

Well, if you'll excuse me, I should be going now.

Introducing a Successor

People will appreciate it if you call on them when you change jobs or positions. If you introduce your successor at the same time, you will ease their transition into their new job.

MICHAEL:

Kondo hongoku ni kaeru koto ni narimashita. Zainichi-chū wa iro-iro to o-sewa ni narimashita. Arigatō gozaimashita.

今度、本国に帰ることになりました。在日中はいろいろとお世話になりました。ありがとうございました。

I'll soon be returning (to my country). Thank you for all your help while I've been in Japan.

TAKAHASHI:

Iya, odorokimashita ne. De, dochira e?

いや、驚きましたね。で、どちらへ?

Well, that's a surprise. And where are you moving to?

MICHAEL:

Nyū Yōku no honsha ni modorimasu ga, kyō, kōnin no Jonson no go-shōkai ni ukagaimashita. Watakushi dōyō yoroshiku o-negai itashimasu.

ニューヨークの本社に戻りますが、今日、後任のジョンソンのご紹介に伺いました。私同様よろしくお願いいたします。

I'll be returning to the head office in New York. I've called today to introduce my successor, Mr. Johnson. I hope you will be as kind to him as you have been to me.

TAKAHASHI:

Hajimemashite. Takahashi desu.

はじめまして。高橋です。

How do you do? My name is Takahashi.

SUCCESSOR:

**Jonson to moshimasu. Tērā no kōnin to shite mairimashita.
Yoroshiku o-negai itashimasu.**

ジョンソンと申します。テーラーの後任としてまいりまし
た。よろしくお願いいたします。

*My name is Johnson and I've come as Taylor's successor. Glad
to meet you.*

TAKAHASHI:

Ima made dō iu o-shigoto o saretan' desu ka?

今までどういうお仕事をされたんですか。

What kind of work were you doing before you came here?

JOHNSON :

Honsha de kenkyū kaihatsu o tantō shite imashita.

本社で研究開発を担当していました。

I was in charge of research and development at head office.

MICHAEL: (when leaving)

**Iro-iro arigatō gozaimashita. Hashimoto shachō ni mo yoro-
shiku o-tsutae kudasai.**

いろいろありがとうございました。橋本社長にもよろしくお
伝えください。

*Thank you for everything. Please give my regards to the president,
Mr. Hashimoto.*

TAKAHASHI:

**Wakarimashita. O-karada o taisetsu ni. Nihon ni koraretara
mata o-yori kudasai. Itsudemo kangei shimasu.**

分かりました。お体を大切に。日本に来られたら、またお
寄りください。いつでも歓迎します。

*I will. Please take care of yourself and when you visit Japan, come
in and see us again. You're always welcome.*

7.09 Seniority in a Company

Although companies are moving away from traditional titles and using terms like "manager" and "leader", here for your reference is a list of traditional titles in order of seniority. A senior managing director, managing director, and, in a large corporation, even a director may have the authority of a vice-president in a US company. The word **torishimariyaku** (取締役) before the title means that the person is a board member.

kaichō	会長	*chairman*
shachō	社長	*chief executive officer, president*
fuku-shachō	副社長	*executive vice-president*
senmu	専務	*senior managing director*
jōmu	常務	*managing director*
buchō	部長	*director*
jichō	次長	*senior manager*
kachō	課長	*manager*
shunin	主任	*supervisor*
kakarichō	係長	*supervisor*

Below are titles for people who work at an English-conversation school:

- **ei-kaiwa gakkō daihyō / rijichō**
  英会話学校代表 / 理事長
  director (and presumably owner) of an English-conversation school

- **eikaiwa kyōshitsu shunin**
  英会話教室主任
  head teacher of an English conversation school

- **ei-kaiwa kōshi/kyōshi**
英会話講師・教師
teacher of English conversation

Numbers

Mastering Japanese numbers is quite a challenge, especially when it gets to large numbers. The basic units are not thousands and millions but **man** (万, units of 10,000) and **oku** (億, units of 100 million). So, ten million is counted as 1,000 **man** (1,000 times 10,000). And a billion is 10 **oku** (10 times 100 million). A trillion is one **chō** (兆).

100	**hyaku**	百	*one hundred*
1,000	**sen**	千	*one thousand*
10,000	**ichiman**	1万	*ten thousand*
100,000	**jūman**	10万	*one hundred thousand*
1,000,000	**hyakuman**	百万	*one million*
10,000,000	**issenman**	1千万	*ten million*
100,000,000	**ichioku**	1億	*one hundred million*
1,000,000,000	**jūoku**	十億	*one billion*
10,000,000,000	**hyakuoku**	百億	*ten billion*
100,000,000,000	**sen'oku**	千億	*one hundred billion*
1,000,000,000,000	**itchō**	1兆	*one trillion*

Polite words

Much used in business, these politer forms of words make the speech sound more sophisticated and professional.

Ordinary form	Polite form	Meaning
kore	**kochira**	this
sore	**sochira**	that

dore	dochira	which
dare	dochira	who
naze	dōshite	why
dō	ikaga	how
otoko no hito, onna no hito	otoko no kata , onna no kata 男の人、女の人	man, woman
(anata no) kaisha	onsha 御社	your company
(uchi no) kaisha	heisha 弊社	our company
isogashii	go-tabō ご多忙	busy

7.10 Words and Expressions

torihiki	取引	*business, transactions, dealings*
torihikisaki	取引先	*clients*
keiei	経営	*management*
meishi	名詞	*business card*
aisatsu	挨拶	*courtesy call*
ōsetsushitsu	応接室	*reception room*
kaigi	会議	*meeting*
nenmatsu no go-aisatsu	年末のご挨拶	*year-end courtesy call*
nenshi no go-aisatsu	年始のご挨拶	*New Year courtesy call*
nagai tsukiai	長い付き合い	*long-standing relationship*
kōshō (suru)	交渉 (する)	*negotiations (to negotiate)*
hinshitsu	品質	*quality*
akaji	赤字	*deficit, in the red*

kuroji	黒字	*surplus, in the black*
tōshi	投資	*investment*
setsubi tōshi	設備投資	*capital spending*
bōnenkai	忘年会	*year end party (office Christmas party)*

Tono-sama Shōbai　殿様商売
"Feudal Lord's Business"

This describes a businessperson who expects their products to sell by themselves. It used to be used to refer to foreign firms that didn't try hard enough to sell their products in Japan's competitive market.

Kaban-mochi　かばん持ち
"Bag-carrier"

This is the person who does all the hard work but is only second in command. If someone says, **Watashi wa kaban-mochi desu kara** (「私はかばん持ちですから」I'm only the bag carrier) this means the speaker does not have the authority to make final decisions.

Chapter 8 Entertaining

Entertaining

Japanese hospitality is legendary, and first-time visitors can be overwhelmed by the hospitality of their Japanese hosts. At one level, there may be fast-paced drinking, moving from, say, an eatery to a bar, and finishing off with karaoke. At another level the guest is offered every kind of food and drink. Whereas in the West we like to ask our guests what they would like (Coffee or tea?), a good host in Japan tries to anticipate guests' needs and provide what they feel is appropriate. So if you're invited to a business dinner you'll probably find that the menu has been arranged in advance and you are plied with different drinks so you will find nothing wanting. The converse is that, especially in the old days, Japanese did not feel comfortable being given a fancy Western menu and asked to choose. There is a scene in the film *Tampopo* (**Itami Juzo**) with a funny take on this.

Beer, **shōchū**, and cold saké are the most popular alcoholic drinks. Pick up your glass when it is being filled and then fill the glass of the other person. Strictly speaking, you're not supposed to pour your own drink. So be on the alert to keep a VIP's glass filled. On the other hand, some people will fill another's glass in order to get a refill themselves, so if your glass is contantly being topped up, it may simply mean that your partner wants more to drink!

At a large party you might find that after the speeches, people move around pouring drinks for others. If there is someone you know or someone important to your company, you should go over and pour that person a drink—sooner rather than later.

When you're invited out, do try to arrive on time. If you realize you're going to be late, phone ahead and ask people to start without you. Otherwise, you might be embarrassed to find that everyone had been waiting for you to arrive before saying "kanpai" and starting the drinking. If you're hosting the meal, get there early, before your guests, and decide on the seating. The person who pays sits near the door. The guests sit on the other side (in a **tatami** room this is in front of the alcove with its scroll and flowers). A typical dinner starts with hors d'oeuvres and beer, and continues with sashimi, tempura, and fish and/or meat dishes with saké, more beer or wine. Rice, or sometimes noodles, mark the end of the meal and the drinking.

You should not worry that you are being rude if you turn down food; in fact, the Japanese themselves do not feel obligated to eat all that's offered. To be polite, you can comment on the food's appearance and be flattered by the number of dishes, but it is all right if you only eat what you like. (Incidentally, children are taught not to start a dish— **hashi o tsukenai**—if they cannot eat the whole portion.)

Customs about who pays the bill are no different from those in most other countries. In business entertaining, whoever issued the invitation generally picks up the tab. When friends go out, the bill is usually split, although sometimes an older person will insist on paying. Private parties are often on a shared-cost basis with guests paying a set contribution made known when the invitation is given.

Vegetarians or those requiring special diets may face difficulties in Japan since such food issues are not widely understood. The prevalence of **katsuobushi** (bonito) stock in otherwise vegan dishes is a common problem. On the other hand, there is a high awareness of genetic modification and soybeans and tofu in Japan are generally from non-GM sources. If you're interested in special diets, look into two home-grown vegetarian diets, the Zen diet (**shōjin ryōri**), and the macrobiotic diet.

In traditional home entertaining, the wife was kept so busy in the kitchen that she did not eat with the guests. Nowadays, people entertain friends at home often with informal cook-at-the-table meals. If you like entertaining at home, remember that late-night dining is not common. You may find your plans for drinks, a leisurely dinner, and discussions late into the night scotched by your Japanese guests arriving punctually, expecting their dinner within half an hour, and leaving early for the long journey home. Also, if you invite people for afternoon tea, make sure they understand that you will be offering them only tea. Otherwise, they may arrive expecting dinner.

When you entertain, you may come up against what is known as **enryo** (reserve and hesitancy), the mark of a good guest in Japanese culture. Even though you urge them to make themselves at home, your Japanese guests may not start drinking or eating until you specifically ask them to start. In some rural districts, people have to be invited three times before they take a sip of their tea!

One more thing you might experience is guests accepting invitations and then not showing up. Although things are changing, work takes precedence and attending private parties may receive low priority.

In spite of these problems, home entertaining can be an enjoyable way to get to know people better. Your friends and acquaintances will certainly appreciate being invited to spend time with you and your family and sample the cuisine of your home country.

8.01   Inviting People

Here are some phrases to use on the phone when you want to get people together. First, Lin asks a friend to a party to celebrate Takuya's recovery:

- **Takuya no kaiki-iwai o jūyokka ni suru yotei nan' da kedo, ko-reru ka na? Basho wa Shiraboshi.**

  拓也の快気祝いを14日にする予定なんだけど、来れるか
  な。場所はしらぼし。

  *I'm planning a celebration for Takuya's recovery. Can you come?
  It's at Shiraboshi (The White Star).*

Next, Kim asks a woman friend to a birthday party she's planning at
her home for her friend Yumi:

- **Yumi-san no tanjōbi dakara, jūrokunichi ni uchi de o-iwai o
  suru yotei na no. Irassharanai? Ryōri o mochiyori ni shiyō to
  omotte.**

  有美さんの誕生日だから、16日に家でお祝いをする予定な
  の。いらっしゃらない？ 料理を持ち寄りにしようと思って。

  *It's Yumi's birthday so I'm planning a celebration on the 16th at
  my place. Won't you come? I'm thinking of a potluck supper.*

The language in this next example is a bit more formal. Emily telephones a friend to ask her and her husband to dinner at a restaurant:

- **Amerika kara gakusei jidai no yūjin ga Nihon ni kite imasu
  keredo, moshi yokattara, jūku-nichi no doyōbi, o-futari de
  yūshoku o issho ni shimasen ka? Ato de kaijō o oshiemasu.**

  アメリカから学生時代の友人が日本に来ていますすけれ
  ど、もしよかったら、19日の土曜日、お二人で夕食を一緒に
  しませんか。後で会場を教えます。

  *Some friends from our student days are over from the States. If
  it's all right with you, we'd like you to join us for dinner on Saturday, the 19th. I'll let you know the place later.*

8.02

Confirming an Invitation

You might want to confirm such an invitation by e-mail:

送信者　　　：〈e.taylor@nifty.com〉
宛先　　　　：〈y.suzuki@ocn.ne.jp〉
送信日時　　：〈2011年4月25日　17.10〉
件名　　　　：19日の件

こんにちは、お元気ですか？　今日は良く晴れて
暖かい一日でしたね。
先日お話した19日の会ですが、日時会場が決まりました
ので、お知らせします。

日時　　　　　　5月19日 (土) 7時より
会場　　　　　　ホテル銀座　フランス料理　シェーヌー
出席メンバー　　テーラー家族全員、ジョンとセーラグリーン夫
　　　　　　　　妻　鈴木ご夫妻

詳しい事は又近いうちに地図等お送りします。

Sōshinsha　　：<e.taylor@nifty.com>
Atesaki　　　：<y.suzuki@ ocn.ne.jp>
Sōshinnichiji：<Nisen jūichi nen shigatsu nijūgo-nichi 17.10>
Kenmei　　　：Jūku-nichi no ken

**Konnichi wa, o-genki desu ka? Kyō wa yoku harete atatakai
ichinichi deshita ne. Senjitsu o-hanashi shita jūrokunichi
no kai desu ga, nichiji, kaijō ga kimarimashita no de, o-shirase
shimasu.**

Nichiji　　　　Gogatsu jūkunichi (do) Shichiji yori
Kaijō　　　　　Hoteru Ginza Furansu ryōri She Nu
Shusseki menbā　Tērā kazoku zenin, Jon to Sēra Guriin fusai
　　　　　　　　　　Suzuki go-fusai

Kuwashii koto wa mata chikai uchi ni chizu tō o-okuri shimasu.

Sender   : <e.taylor@nifty.com>
Recipient : <y.suzuki@ ocn.ne.jp>
Date sent : <25 April 2011   17.10>
Subject   : Re: 19th

Hi, how are you? It was a sunny warm day today, wasn't it? About the party on the 19th we talked about the other day, the place and time have been decided so this is to let you know.

Date and time   May 19th (Saturday) From 7 p.m.
Place   Hotel Ginza, French restaurant, Chez Nous
People attending All the Taylor family, Mr and Mrs John and Sarah Green and Mr and Mrs Suzuki

As for the details, I'll send a map etc. soon.

8.03   Declining an Invitation

A man declines an invitation from a close friend:

- **Arigatō. Warui kedo, sono hi ni yotei ga arun' da yo.**
  ありがとう、悪いけど、その日に予定があるんだよ。
  Thanks. I'm sorry but I've got something on that day.

A politer way to say the same thing is:

- **Arigatō gozaimasu. Zannen desu ga, sono hi ni chotto yotei ga arimashite, mōshiwake arimasen.**
  ありがとうございます。残念ですが、その日にちょっと予定がありまして、申し訳ありません。
  Thank you. Unfortunately I have something to do that day. I'm sorry.

Here's how to refuse an invitation you've already accepted:

- **Ashita no yakusoku no koto desu kedo. Kyūyō ga dekite, shus-seki dekinaku nattan' desu yo. Hontō ni zannen desu ga.**
  明日の約束のことですけど。急用ができて、出席できなくなったんですよ。本当に残念ですが。
  It's about our appointment tomorrow. Something urgent has cropped up and I won't be able to come. I'm very sorry.

8.04 Receiving Guests at Home

You will need a clear policy on shoes. If you wear shoes in your home, tell guests to treat your house like a hotel. If you have a shoes-off policy, line up house slippers in the entranceway before the guests arrive. Here are a few phrases you can use to make your guests feel at home.

- **O-machi shite imashita. Dōzo.**
  お待ちしていました。どうぞ。
  We've been expecting you. Please come in.

- **Dōzo, o-agari kudasai.**
  どうぞ、お上がりください。
  Please come in. (lit. Please come up.)

- **Irasshai!**
  いらっしゃい。
  Welcome! (used especially for unexpected guests)

- **Kutsu no mama, dōzo.**
  靴のまま、どうぞ。
  Please keep your shoes on.

- **Dōzo kochira e. Michi wa sugu wakarimashita ka?**
  どうぞ、こちらへ。道はすぐ分かりましたか。
  Please come this way. Did you find your way easily?

- **Chotto o-machi kudasai. Kōhii o motte kimasu kara.**
  ちょっとお待ちください。コーヒーを持ってきますから。
  Just a moment. I'll get some coffee.

- **O-cha, dōzo.**
  お茶どうぞ。
  Please have some tea. / Please go ahead and drink your tea.

- **Yoroshikattara kukkii o dōzo. Tezukuri desu.**
  よろしかったらクッキーをどうぞ。手作りです。
  Please try a cookie. They're home made.

8.05 Visiting Someone's Home

When you reach the house, ring the bell and announce your name through the interphone. In the old days, when doors were not locked, you would slide the door open and announce your arrival with a loud "**Gomen kudasai.**"

Leave your shoes neatly lined up in the entranceway. Strictly speaking, you should leave your shoes facing toward the inside of the house, and at some point during your stay they would be turned around to face the outside, ready for leaving (apparently because it was bad form to back up into a house). These days most people turn their shoes around when entering the house.

When you're a guest, here are some phrases you can use:

- **Shitsurei shimasu / O-jama shimasu.**
  失礼します ／ お邪魔します。
  Excuse me (say this when you take your shoes off and again when you enter the living room).

- **O-isogashii tokoro, arigatō gozaimashita.**
  お忙しいところ、ありがとうございました。
  Thank you for making time to see us.

- **Dōzo, o-kamai naku.**
  どうぞ、お構いなく。
  Please don't go to any trouble (when offered tea or drinks).

- **Unten dakara, o-sake wa nomimasen. Ūroncha de mo itadakemasen ka?**
  運転だから、お酒は飲みません。ウーロン茶でもいただけませんか。
  I'm driving so I won't drink. Could I have some Oolong tea?

- **Sumimasen. O-tearai o o-kari shitain' desu ga.**
  すみません。お手洗いをお借りしたいんですが。
  May I use the bathroom?

- **Ii o-sumai desu ne.**
  いいお住まいですね。
  What a nice place you have.

- **Suteki na chawan desu ne. Hagi deshō ka?**
  すてきな茶碗ですね。萩でしょうか。
  What a beautiful teacup! Is it Hagi pottery?

8.06 Having Friends to Dinner

Max and Kate Brown have invited the Okadas who run the English school where Max teaches to dinner at their home. The Okadas don't speak much English so Kate and Max are doing their best to impress and make them feel at home.

KATE:

> **O-shokuji no yōi ga dekimashita no de, dōzo.**
> **Dōzo o-meshiagari kudasai.**
> お食事の用意ができましたので、どうぞ。
> どうぞお召し上がりください。

Dinner's ready. Please (come to the table).
Please go ahead and start.

EVERYONE:

Itadakimasu.
いただきます。
Bon appetit. (lit. I receive.)

KATE:

Dōzo, o-tori kudasai. Yōshoku wa o-kuchi ni aimasu ka?
どうぞ、お取りください。洋食はお口に合いますか。
Please help yourself. Do you like Western food?

MRS OKADA:

Ē. Sappari shite oishii desu ne.
えー。さっぱりしておいしいですね。
Yes, it's light and very delicious.

KATE:

Yasai wa hōfu de shinsen. Nihon no seikatsu wa hontō ni benri de, chian mo yokute, sumiyasui desu ne. Kazoku minna ga sukkari kochira no seikatsu ni najinde,
野菜は豊富で新鮮。日本の生活はほんとうに便利で、治安もよくて、住みやすいですね。家族皆がすっかりこちらの生活になじんで。
Vegetables are so abundant and fresh. Life in Japan is really convenient, and safe. It's easy to live here. The whole family has got completely used to life here.

MAX:

Mō shibaraku Nihon ni itai to kangaete imasu ga, shigoto no hō wa?
もうしばらく日本にいたいと考えていますが、仕事の方は？
I'm thinking of staying in Japan a bit longer, but what about work?

OKADA:

Ite kureru to tasukaru yo. Anata hodo ninki no aru sensei wa metta ni imasen yo.

いてくれると助かるよ。あなたほど人気のある先生はめったにいませんよ。

If you could stay on that would be a help. It's not often (you find) a teacher who's as popular as you are.

MAX:

Arigatō gozaimasu. Sore de wa, sono hōkō de. Hanashi ga kawarimasu ga, saikin sugoi hakken. Eki no higashiguchi atari ni monosugoku oishii yakitoriya.

ありがとうございます。それでは、その方向で。話が変わりますが、最近すごい発見。駅の東口あたりにものすごくおいしい焼き鳥屋。

Thank you. Well then, (we'll go) in that direction. On a different matter, I recently made a great discovery. In the area near the east exit of the station, an incredibly good yakitori place ...

KATE:

Okada-san, mō sukoshi ikaga desu ka?

岡田さん、もう少しいかがですか。

Mr Okada, how about a little more?

OKADA:

Iya, kekkō desu. Takusan itadakimashita. Gochiso-sama deshita.

いや、結構です。たくさんいただきました。ご馳走様でした。

No more, thank you. I've had a lot to eat. Thank you.

8.07

Taking Clients Out to Dinner

EcoSystems's talks with Mr Takahashi and his colleagues are going well and Michael has decided to take them out to dinner. He wants to give them a good time and try to get to know them better.

MICHAEL:

Mazu, biiru ni shimashō ka? Nama biiru yottsu kudasai. Kanpai!
まず、ビールにしましょうか。生ビール4つください。カンパイ！
To start with shall we have some beer? Four draught beers, please. Cheers!

SATO YUMI:

Aa, natsu wa biiru ni kagiru. De mo, buchō no go-shusshin no Kyūshū wa mōshō rashii desu ne.
ああ、夏はビールに限る。でも、部長のご出身の九州は、猛暑らしいですね。
Ah, beer is the best drink in summer. But, it seems to be extremely hot in Kyushu where you come from.

TAKAHASHI:

Atsukute tamaranai desu yo. Sono ippō, fuyu wa kaiteki. Maikeru-san wa ryokō suru to ii desu yo. Nagasaki, Aso-san, Hakata. Meibutsu no sakana, shōchū.
暑くてたまらないですよ。その一方、冬は快適。マイケルさんは旅行するといいですよ。長崎、阿蘇山、博多。名物の魚、焼酎。
It's dreadfully hot. On the other hand, it's pleasant in winter. You should take a trip. Nagasaki, Mt Aso, Hakata. It's famous for its fish, its shōchū.

MICHAEL:

Shōjiki itte, Kōbe yori nishi e itta koto ga nai desu yo. Iku beki desu yo ne.

正直言って、神戸より西へ行ったことがないですよ。行くべきですよね。

To tell you the truth, I've never been west of Kobe. I probably should go.

TAKAHASHI:

Ikanai wake ni wa ikanai desu yo. Sono setsu, go-annai shimasu yo.

行かないわけにはいかないですよ。その節、ご案内しますよ。

You simply must go. And when you do, I'll show you round.

MICHAEL:

Sā sā, Nihonshu ikimashō ka. Soretomo, buchō no go shusshinchi no shōchū de mo. Imo-shōchū ga ii desu ka, mugishōchū ga ii desu ka. O-susume no mono arimasen ka.

さあさあ、日本酒、いきましょうか。それとも、部長のご出身地の焼酎でも。芋焼酎がいいですか、麦焼酎の方がいいですか。おすすめのものありませんか。

Well, shall we have some sake? Or, some shōchū from where you come from? Which is better, potato shōchū or barley shōchū? Is there one you can recommend?

8.08 Taking Friends Out to Dinner

Michael and Emily's college friends are visiting from the States. John and Sarah have various food issues that have to be explained to the chef.

WAITER:

Irasshaimase! O-machi shite orimashita. Dōzo kochira e.

いらっしゃいませ。お待ちしておりました。どうぞ、こちらへ。

Welcome. We've been waiting for you. This way, please.

EMILY:

Sumimasen. Kochira no futari wa bejitarian de, kochira no kata ni wa gyūnyū arerugii ga arimasu. Anshin shite tabe-rareru menyū o oshiete kudasai.

すみません。こちらの二人はベジタリアンで、こちらの方には牛乳アレルギーがあります。安心して食べられるメニューを教えてください。

Excuse me. We have two vegetarians and this person has an allergy to milk. Can you tell me what from the menu they would be able to eat with peace of mind?

WAITER:

Bejitarian no kata wa niku mo sakana mo meshiagaranai wake desu ne.

ベジタリアンの方は肉も魚も召し上がらないわけですね。

You mean the vegetarians eat neither fish nor meat.

EMILY:

Hai, issai dame desu. Dashi ni haitte mo dame desu. Ageda-shidōfu wa oishisō desu ga, katsuobushi no dashi tsukatte imasu ka.

はい、一切だめです。だしに入ってもだめです。揚げ出し豆腐はおいしそうですが、かつおぶしのだしを使っていますか。

That's right, none at all. None in the stock either. This deep-fried tofu looks good but do you use bonito stock?

WAITER:

Goma dake no sōsu mo dekimasu.

ゴマだけのソースもできます。

We can give you a sauce with only sesame in it.

EMILY:

Sore o mittsu kudasai.

それを三つください。後は？

Three of those please. What else (do you have)?

WAITER:

Kochira no itamemono wa niku-nuki de o-dashi dekimasu. Ato wa tōnyu chiizu no pizza mo gozaimasu shi, genmai no kinoko rizotto ga gozaimasu. Pasutarui wa o-konomi ni awasete o-tsukuri dekimasu.

こちらの炒め物は肉抜きでお出しできます。後は、豆乳チーズのピザもございますし、玄米のきのこリゾットがございます。パスタ類はお好みに合わせてお作りできます。

We can make these stir-fried dishes without meat. Then there is a soy milk cheese pizza and a brown rice mushroom risotto. We can make any of the pastas as you please.

8.09 Special Diets

Describing any special dietary needs, particularly vegetarianism, may test your Japanese simply because many people are not familiar with the issues. The vocabulary itself is easy as many of the terms are from the English.

bejitarian	ベジタリアン	*vegetarian*
bigan	ヴィガン	*vegan*
ōganikku	オーガニック	*organic*

This is a hard one though:

idenshi kumikae daizu	遺伝子組み換え 大豆	*genetically modified soybean*

Food allergies (**shokumotsu arerugii** 食物アレルギー) are more common and the Japanese government requires labelling for seven of the most common allergens:

tamago	卵	*egg*
nyūseihin	乳製品	*dairy products*
komugi	小麦	*wheat*
ebi	えび	*shrimp*
kani	かに	*crab*
rakkasei	落花生	*peanut*
soba	そば	*buckwheat*

In addition there are recommendations for the labelling of 18 more, including **daizu** (大豆 soybean). The Japanese for cross-contamination is simply **kontaminēshon** (コンタミネーション). MSG (**gurutaminsan** グルタミン酸) is more commonly known by its brand name Aji no Moto.

8.10 Taking Your Leave

When it's time to go, look at your watch and say the magic words, **Mō, soro-soro** (もう、そろそろ It's about time to go) which will immediately signal that you want to leave. Out of politeness, your host will probably try at least once to detain you.

OKADA:

> **Dōmo, o-jama shimashita. Taihen gochisō ni narimashita.**
> どうも、お邪魔しました。たいへんご馳走になりました。
> *Thank you for having us over. (lit. We're sorry to have bothered you.) And thank you for the meal.*

MAX:

> **Mada iin' ja nain' desu ka?**
> まだいいんじゃないですか?
> *Can't you stay longer?*

OKADA:

> **Ashita hayai mon' desu kara.**
> 明日早いもんですから。
> *I have to be up early tomorrow morning.*

KATE:

> **Sore-dewa, zehi mata o-dekake kudasai.**
> それでは、ぜひまたお出かけください。
> *Then please come again.*

These phrases can also be used when you leave:

- **Osoku made, o-jama shite wa mōshi-wake arimasen kara.**
  遅くまでお邪魔しては申し訳ありませんから。
  I don't want to keep you up late.

- **Sono-uchi, mata yukkuri o-jama shimasu.**
  そのうち、またゆっくりお邪魔します。
  I'll stay longer next time I come.

- **Dōzo kondo wa uchi ni oide kudasai**
  どうぞ、今度はうちにおいでください。
  Come and visit us next time.

- **O-saki ni shitsurei shimasu.**
  お先に失礼します。
  Excuse me but I've got to go (said to the other guests).

8.11   Words and Expressions

izakaya	居酒屋	*bar*
resutoran	レストラン	*restaurant*
ryōtei	料亭	*traditional (and expensive) Japanese restaurant*
kanpai	乾杯	*Cheers!*
nama biiru	生ビール	*draught beer*
reishu	冷酒	*cold sake*
shōchū	焼酎	*Spirit made from potatoes or barley served on ice, with hot water or as a cocktail*
motenashi	もてなし	*hospitality*
settai (suru)	接待 (する)	*entertaining (usually business), to entertain*
shōtai (suru)	招待 (する)	*invitation, to invite*
tsukiai	付き合い	*association, acquaintance, friendship*

resepushon	レセプション	*reception*
enkai	宴会	*party, usually in a tatami room*
zashiki	座敷	*big tatami room used for parties*
baikingu	バイキング	*help-yourself buffet*
hōmu pātei	ホームパーテイ	*party held at home*
nijikai	二次会	*party held immediately after another party*
o-aisō	おあいそう	*bill in sushi bars and Japanese restaurants*
o-kanjō	お勘定	*bill in other restaurants*
kaihi	会費	*set contribution to a party*
shokuji o ogoru	食事をおごる	*to treat someone to a meal*
karaoke	カラオケ	*karaoke*
gozen-sama	午前様	*person who comes home after midnight*

Chapter 9 Children

Children

Japan's low birth rate is cause for concern. It has been declining steadily since the late 1970s. By 2009, the birth rate had dropped to1.32 births per woman, well below the replacement rate needed to maintain the population level. Women delaying marriage and more people, both men and women, remaining single are the main reasons, but the background to these lifestyle changes is complex. Twenty years of recession, with more workers on contracts and low incomes, have caused many people to worry about the expense of raising a family, and about their children's future. Then, there are the problems of working while child-rearing—for example, the lack of affordable child care, the obstacles involved in getting back into work, and a lack of support for mothers and families generally. There is now a special government minister and legislation to promote "work-life balance" but the problems require far-reaching social change and so far these measures have failed to halt the decline.

So what kind of child care is available? At the pre-school level there are nurseries (**hoikuen**) which accept babies from a few months and provide child care until school age for a full working day, and kinder-gartens (**yōchien**) which take children for one, two, or three years before starting grade school; but it's a short day, with children return-ing home either at lunch time or early afternoon (many do, however, extend care until 5 PM or so). The learning environment at Japanese nurseries and kindergartens is positive and cheerful, structured and well-organized, and the staff are infinitely patient. Lunches are healthy (although you may have difficulty trying to control diet allergies). At some kindergartens you may have to make **bentō**, a boxed lunch, every day and this is no easy task as the competition from other parents for the most colorful, original **bentō** can be stiff!

A Japanese kindergarten can teach your child Japanese, provide Japanese friends for the whole family, and give you an opportunity to see Japanese society from the inside. You may, however, have to resolve unexpected problems. For example, because Japanese schools often expect mothers to help out in various ways, you might not have as much free time as you anticipated. Also, you might feel pressure to conform; for instance, you may have to let your child take more sweets than you would like on a school outing. You will have to come to terms too with the emphasis on group activity.

To Westerners, Japanese parents seem indulgent, and to Japanese, Western parents seem strict. The Western parent teaches children to recognize social situations and to behave appropriately; having set down the rules, the parent usually does not tolerate children who disobey. On the other hand, the Japanese parent trains not by principle but by example. The child may not obey at first, but the parent knows that he or she eventually will. You'll also find that some Japanese parents sleep with their infants (a custom called **soine**) rather than put them in a cot, and share the bath until the child is well into grade school, the emphasis being on "skinship" rather than on teaching independence.

Because Japanese parents' scholastic expectations are high, many children commute to **juku**, private tutoring schools offering classes after regular school hours and on weekends. **Juku** can be a good place for foreign children to learn to read and write Japanese, and also improve in other areas like arithmetic. Virtually every neighborhood has teachers of piano, English, and abacus, and not far away there will surely be facilities for judo, kendo, ballet, violin, swimming, gymnastics, and many other activities. Fees are generally reasonable but they can mount up if you have several children taking two or three courses.

Compulsory education in Japan is for nine years: six years of elementary school followed by three years of junior high. All elementary and junior high schools follow a standard curriculum set down by the Ministry of Education. When Japanese children go to junior high they become increasingly involved with school-related activities. Students stay on after school to attend semi-compulsory clubs that can keep them out of the house for up to twelve hours a day.

Although children have a less rigid schedule than in the past, the system is still geared to preparing students for exams, partly because graduation from a good university offers the best chance of a job with a top-ranked company. But entrance exams are not limited to universities; exams for entering high school, junior high school and even grade school are common, especially in the private sector.

Prior to exams, family members go out of their way to give the student the best conditions for studying. Summer vacations may be forgone and Christmas and New Year celebrations abbreviated because someone is taking full-time courses to prepare for these exams. As the February exam season approaches, mothers serve warming snacks to tide their children through the late-night cramming, and TV programs give advice on how to avoid colds that could jeopardize this chance of a lifetime. Entrance into university marks the culmination of a long, intense scholastic endeavor, and college days tend to be a happy, carefree hiatus before the reality of looking for a job and starting working life.

9.01 Child's Play

The rough and tumble of children's play knows no language barrier, but teaching these basic words to your toddler can help ease his or her way into Japanese infant society.

• **irete/mazete**	入れて・まぜて	*Can I join in?*
• **kashite**	貸して	*Can I borrow this?*
• **junban da yo**	順番だよ	*Take turns!*
• **arigatō**	ありがとう	*Thanks*
• **dame**	ダメ	*No, you can't*
• **gomen-nasai**	ごめんなさい	*Sorry*
• **zurui/ijiwaru**	ずるい・いじわる	*Not fair*

These phrases are for parents:

• **o-namae wa?**	お名前は？	*What's your name?*
• **ikutsu / nansai?**	いくつ / 何歳？	*How old are you?*
• **o-rikō-san**	お利口さん	*That's a good boy/girl*

9.02

Admiring a Baby

In this dialogue, Kim Young Hee admires a neighbor's baby.

KIM:

Kawaii desu ne. Ōkiku narimashita ne. Ima nankagetsu?
かわいいですね。大きくなりましたね。今、何ヶ月？
Isn't she cute! Hasn't she grown. How old is she now?

NEIGHBOR:

Jukkagetsu.
10ヶ月。
Ten months.

KIM:

Sō. Otōsan ni nite imasu ne.
そう。お父さんに似ていますね。
Really? Doesn't she look like her father!

NEIGHBOR:

Ē, minna ni iwarerun' desu.
えー、皆に言われるんです。
Yes, everyone says so.

KIM:

Rinyū-shoku wa?
離乳食は？
How's the weaning going?

NEIGHBOR:

Gohan, o-tōfu, o-sakana o takusan tabete, kudamono mo daisuki desu.
ご飯、お豆腐、お魚をたくさん食べて、果物も大好きです。
She eats a lot of rice, tofu, and fish, and she loves fruit.

KIM:

Yokatta desu ne. Shigoto ni fukki shimasu ka?
よかったですね。仕事に復帰しますか？
That's good. Are you going back to work?

NEIGHBOR:

Hai, yōyaku hoikuen o mitsukete, raigetsu kara kaisha ni mo-doru yotei na no.
はい、ようやく保育園を見つけて、来月から会社に戻る予定なの。
Yes, at last I found (a place in) a nursery and I plan to go back to work next month.

KIM:

Ryōritsu wa taihen desu kara, ganbatte kudasai.
両立はたいへんですから、がんばってください。
It's hard doing both (working and parenting). Good luck.

9.03 Asking About a Kindergarten

Some kindergartens are run by local authorities, but the majority are privately owned. Most do not give formal training in reading and arithmetic. Since it looks as if they'll be staying longer in Japan, Kate asks a neighbor about the age requirements for a local kindergarten.

KATE:

Megumi-chan wa doko no yōchi-en e kayotte irun' desu ka?
恵ちゃんはどこの幼稚園へ通っているんですか。
Which kindergarten does Megumi go to?

NEIGHBOR:

Akebono Yōchi-en. Jinja no yōchi-en na no.

あけぼの幼稚園。神社の幼稚園なの。

Akebono (Dawn) Kindergarten. It's run by a Shinto shrine.

KATE:

Uchi no Ken wa haireru ka na?

うちのケンは入れるかな？

Could our Ken go there?

NEIGHBOR:

O-tanjōbi wa itsu?

お誕生日はいつ？

When's his birthday?

KATE:

Jūnigatsu ni yon-sai ni naru no.

12月に4歳になるの。

He'll be four in December.

NEIGHBOR:

San-nen hoiku ni narimasu ne. Kiite mitara dō desu ka? Ima, Megumi o mukae ni ikimasu kara issho ni ikanai?

3年保育になりますね。聞いてみたらどうですか。今、恵みを向かえに行きますから一緒に行かない？

Then he would go for three years. Why don't you ask? I'm going to meet Megumi now so why don't you come along?

KATE:

Hai. Arigatō gozaimasu.

はい、ありがとうございます。

OK. Thank you.

9.04　Introducing Yourself

If you have children attending a Japanese school, you may be asked to introduce yourself at class meetings. You can use the following, conventionally modest introduction:

- **Erena Tērā no haha desu. Sannen-mae, Amerika kara mairimashita. Kodomo wa mada Nihongo o yoku hanasemasen shi, narenai koto ga ōi ka to omoimasu ga, yoroshiku o-negai shimasu.**
  エレナ・テーラーの母です。3年前、アメリカから参りました。子供はまだ日本語をよく話せませんし、なれないことが多いかと思いますが、よろしくお願いいたします。
  I am Eleanor Taylor's mother. We came from America three years ago. Eleanor still does not speak Japanese well and I think there are lots of things she hasn't gotten used to yet. I would appreciate it if you would look after her.

9.05　Telephoning the School

Max telephones the kindergarten to tell them that Ken is sick and will be absent from class.

TEACHER:

> **Hai. Akebono Yōchien desu.**
> はい。あけぼの幼稚園です。
> *Hello. Akebono Kindergarten.*

MAX:

> **Kiku gumi no Ken Buraun no chichi desu.**
> 菊組みのケン・ブラウンの父です。
> *This is Ken Brown's father. Ken's in the "chrysanthemum" class.*

TEACHER:

Hai.
はい。
Yes.

MAX:

Kodomo ga netsu o dashimashita node, kyō wa yasumasetai to omoimasu.
子供が熱を出しましたので、今日は休ませたいと思います。
Ken's got a temperature so I'd like to keep him out of school today.

TEACHER:

Wakarimashita. O-daiji ni.
分かりました。お大事に。
I see. I hope he feels better.

MAX:

Yoroshiku o-negai shimasu. Shitsurei shimasu.
よろしくお願いします。失礼します。
Thank you. Goodbye.

9.06

Writing an Absence Note

If you go away for a long weekend, you'll have to send a note informing the school that your child will be absent.

- **Ashita (kinyōbi) kazoku de dekakeru no de, Erena o yasumasete kudasai.**
  明日(金曜日)家族で出かけるので、エレナを休ませてください。
  Because the family is going out of town, please excuse Eleanor from school tomorrow (Friday).

9.07 Inviting Children to a Party

A good way to get to know the neighbors is to invite their children to a party. When talking to other parents, use the honorific verb **irassharu** when referring to their children.

EMILY:

Nijū-san-nichi ni Kurisumasu pātii o uchi de suru koto ni nat-ta no. Satomi-chan to Kenta-kun, irassharanai? Ato de kādo o kodomo ni motasemasu.

23日にクリスマス・パーテイを家ですることになったの。里美ちゃんと健太君いらっしゃらない?後でカードを子供に持たせます。

We're having a Christmas party on the 23rd. Can Satomi and Kenta come? I'll send the children round later with an invitation.

NEIGHBOR:

Arigatō gozaimasu.
ありがとうございます。
Thank you.

EMILY:

Shimizu-san to Hayashi-san no kodomo-san mo kimasu no de, kite kudasai.
清水さんと林さんの子供さんも来ますので、来てください。
The Shimizu and Hayashi children are coming too, so please come.

NEIGHBOR:

Hai. Dōmo arigatō gozaimasu. Kodomo ga kitto yorokobu deshō.
はい。どうもありがとう。こどもがきっと喜ぶでしょう。
Thank you very much. The children will be delighted.

EMILY:

Zehi, dōzo. O-machi shite imasu.
ぜひ、どうぞ。お待ちしています。
Please come. We look forward to seeing them.

Visiting the Pediatrician

You can take a sick child to a neighborhood pediatrician or to the paediatric ward of a general hospital. You will have to show your insurance card or settle the method of payment before treatment is given.

DOCTOR:

Dō shimashita ka?
どうしましたか。
What's the matter?

MAX:

Kinō no yoru kara netsu o dashimashita.
昨日の夜から熱を出しました。
He's had a fever since last night.

DOCTOR:

Kinō nan-do deshita ka?
昨日何度でしたか。
What was his temperature yesterday?

MAX:

Sanjū-hachi-do nana-bu arimashita.
38度7部ありました。
It was 38.7 degrees centigrade.

DOCTOR:

Geri wa?
下痢は？
Any diarrhea?

MAX:

Geri wa shite inai desu.
下痢はしていないです。
No, no diarrhea.

DOCTOR:

Hakimashita ka?
吐きましたか？
Did he vomit?

MAX:

Iie. Haite imasen.
いいえ、吐いていません。
No, no vomiting.

DOCTOR:

Dewa chotto shinsatsu shimasu ne. * * * Taishita koto nai to omoimasu. Suibun o takusan ataete kudasai. Kaze-gusuri to genetsuzai o dashimasu.
では、ちょっと診察しますね。*** 大したことないと思います。
水分をたくさん与えてください。かぜ薬と解熱剤を出します。
*Let me examine him. * * * I don't think it's anything serious. Give him lots of fluids. I'll give him some medicine for the cold and something to bring the fever down.*

MAX:

Arigatō gozaimashita.
ありがとうございました。
Thank you very much.

9.09

Describing Ailments

You might need to use one of the following phrases to help the doctor understand what is wrong with your child.

- **Nodo / o-naka ga itai.**
  のど / おなかが痛い。
  He has a sore throat / tummy ache.

- **Karada ga darui.**
  体がだるい。
  He feels listless.

- **Hanamizu o dashi, seki o shite, zēzē shite imasu.**
  鼻水をだし、咳をして、ゼーゼーしています。
  She's got a runny nose, a cough and she's wheezing.

- **Piinattsu ga nodo ni tsumatte iru.**
  ピーナツがのどに詰まっている。
  He's got a peanut stuck in his throat.

- **Kaidan kara ochite, te o kitte, atama o utta.**
  階段から落ちて、手を切って、頭を打った。
  He fell down the stairs, cut his hand, and hit his head.

- **Kizetsu shita.**
  気絶した。
  He fainted.

- **Hossa o okoshita.**
  発作を起こした。
  He's had a spasm.

CHILDHOOD ILLNESSES AND MEDICAL TERMS

hentō-sen	扁桃腺	*tonsillitis*
infuruenza	インフルエンザ	*influenza*
chūji-en	中耳炎	*middle ear infection*
kikanshien	気管支炎	*bronchitis*
haien	肺炎	*pneumonia*
hashika	はしか	*measles*
mizubōsō	水ぼうそう	*chicken pox*
otafuku-kaze	おたふくかぜ	*mumps*
fūshin	風疹	*German measles*
shōni zensoku	小児ぜんそく	*infantile asthma*
atopii	アトピー	*atopic dermatitis*
tobihi	飛び火	*impetigo*
Nihon nōen	日本脳炎	*Japanese encephalitis*
hyakunichi-zeki	百日咳	*whooping cough (pertussis)*
jifuteria	ジフテリア	*diphtheria*
hashōfu	はしょうふ	*tetanus*
kossetsu	骨折	*fracture*
kenkō shindan	健康診断	*medical check-up*
yobō sesshu	予防接種	*vaccination*
sanshukongō wakuchin	三種混合ワクチン	*DTP vaccine (diphtheria, pertussis, tetanus)*
shin-sanshukongō wakuchin	新三種混合ワクチン	*MMR vaccine (measles, mumps, rubella)*

9.10 Asking About Swimming Lessons

Many swimming pools offer courses both for adults and for children.
Emily asks about swimming lessons for babies.

EMILY:

Uchi no kodomo ni suiei o sasetain' dakedo, bebii suimingu wa arimasu ka?

家の子供に水泳をさせたいんだけど、ベビースイミングはありますか?

I'd like my child to take swimming lessons. Do you have classes for babies here?

SWIMMING COACH:

Hai, gozaimasu. Kōsu wa getsuyō to mokuyō no jū-ji-han kara jū-ichi-ji made desu.

はい、ございます。コースは月曜と木曜の10時半から11時までです。

Yes, we do. The course is on Mondays and Thursdays from 10:30 to 11:00.

EMILY:

Nankagetsu kara dekimasu ka?

何ヶ月からできますか。

From what age can babies start?

SWIMMING COACH:

Sankagetsu kara desu.

3ヶ月からです。

From three months.

EMILY:

Gessha wa ikura desho ka?

月謝はいくらでしょうか。

How much are the lessons per month?

SWIMMING COACH:

Nyūkai-kin wa yonsen-en, gessha wa gosen-en desu.
入会金は4,000円、月謝は5,000円です。
There's an entrance fee of four thousand yen and then a monthly fee of five thousand yen.

EMILY:

Mizu wa tsumetakunain' desu ka?
水は冷たくないんですか。
Isn't the water cold?

SWIMMING COACH:

Akachan senyō no pūru ga gozaimashite, suion ga itsumo sanjū-ni-do ijō ni natte orimasu. Go-annai shimashō ka?
赤ちゃん専用のプールがございまして、水温がいつも32度以上になっております。ご案内しましょうか。
There's a baby pool where the water is always over 32°. Shall I show you around?

EMILY:

Hai. O-negai shimasu.
はい、お願いします。
Yes, please.

9.11 Meeting Your Child's Teacher

If you notice something wrong with your child's behavior, you can discuss the problem with his or her teacher. You can usually find teachers working in the staff room until the evening.

MICHAEL:

Gomen kudasai. Koizumi Sensei, o-negai shimasu.
ごめんください。小泉先生お願いします。
Excuse me. I'd like to see Mr. Koizumi.

SCHOOL OFFICIAL:

Hai. Shōshō o-machi kudasai.
はい、少々お待ちください。
Yes. Please wait one moment.

MICHAEL: (As teacher approaches)

Itsumo o-sewa ni natte orimasu. Chotto go-sōdan shitai koto ga arimashite. . .
いつもお世話になっております。ちょっとご相談したいことがありまして、
We're much obliged to you. Could I have a word with you?

TEACHER:

Hai. Kyōshitsu e ikimashō. * * * Dewa, dōzo o-hanashi kudasai.
はい、教室へ行きましょう。*** では、どうぞ、お話ください。
*OK. Let's go to the classroom. * * * Well, what would you like to discuss?*

MICHAEL:

Jon ga konogoro shizunde ite, yōsu ga itsumo to chigau mono desu kara, ki ni natte . . .
ジョンがこのごろ沈んでいて、様子がいつもと違うものですから、気になって、
John is depressed these days. He's not the same as usual, so I've been worried.

TEACHER:

Sō desu ka? Kyōshitsu de wa akarukute, benkyō ni hagende imasu. Seiseki mo ii hō da shi, shinpai wa iranai to omoimasu keredomo. Tomodachi to yoku asonde imasu ka?
そうですか。教室では明るくて、勉強に励んでいます。成績もいい方だし、心配はいらないと思いますけれども。友達とよく遊んでいますか。
Is that so? He's cheerful in class and works hard. His marks are above average so I don't think there's need for concern. Does he play with his friends a lot?

MICHAEL:

Iie. Hitori de gēmu de asonde imasu.

いいえ。一人でゲームで遊んでいます。

No. He plays computer games by himself.

TEACHER:

Ja, tomodachi dōshi de nani-ka ga atta no kamo-shiremasen ne. Ashita kiite mimashō.

じゃ、友達同士で何かがあったのかもしれませんね。明日聞いてみましょう。

Then he may have had some trouble with his friends. I'll try to find out tomorrow.

MICHAEL:

O-negai shimasu.

お願いします。

Thank you very much.

TEACHER:

Ato de go-renraku shimasu. Sore kara denwa demo ii desu kara, tsuzukete renraku o toriaimashō.

後で、ご連絡します。それから電話でもいいですから、続けて連絡を取り合いましょう。

I'll contact you later. And, it's all right to phone so let's keep in touch.

9.12 Words and Expressions

SOCIAL

shōshika	少子化	*low birth rate*
ryōritsu	両立	*to be a working mother*

shigoto ni fukki suru	仕事に復帰する	*to return to work*
sankyū	産休	*maternity leave*
ikuji kyūka	育児休暇	*leave for parenting (both mother and father)*

BIRTH

omedeta desu ka?	おめでたですか	*Are you expecting?*
ninshin suru	妊娠する	*to be pregnant*
boshi techō	母子手帳	*mother's pocketbook (medical record kept by mother)*
sanfujinka	産婦人科	*obstetrics and gynecology*
o-san	お産	*birth, delivery*
bunben-shitsu	分娩室	*delivery room*
o-san ni tachiau	お産に立ち会う	*to be present at the birth*

BABIES

bonyū	母乳	*breast-feeding*
miruku	ミルク	*formula, milk preparation*
honyūbin	哺乳瓶	*feeding bottle*
oppai o yaru	おっぱいをやる	*to breastfeed a baby*
oppai o nomu	おっぱいを飲む	*to drink from the breast*
rinyūshoku	離乳食	*weaning, solid food*
kami o-mutsu	紙おむつ	*disposable diapers*
onbu o suru	おんぶをする	*to carry on the back*
dakko o suru	だっこをする	*to carry in the arms*
bagii	バギー	*baby car*
chairudo shiito	チャイルド・シート	*car seat*
komori-uta	子守唄	*lullaby*

PRE-SCHOOL

hoikujo/hoikuen	保育所・保育園	*nursery*
yōchien	幼稚園	*kindergarten*
ensoku	遠足	*school outing*

GRADE SCHOOL

shōgakkō	小学校	*elementary school*
nyūgaku-shiki	入学式	*entrance ceremony*
randoseru	ランドセル	*knapsack, satchel*
tōkō suru	登校する	*to go to school*
kumi	組	*class*
san-nen ichi-kumi	三年一組	*class one of third grade*
sensei	先生	*teacher*
undōkai	運動会	*sports day; field day*
jugyō	授業	*lesson*
sankanbi	参観日	*day when parents watch a class*
kyūshoku	給食	*school lunch*

seisekihyō/tsūshinbo	成績表・通信簿	*report card*
hōkago	放課後	*after-school hours*
o-keiko/naraigoto	お稽古・習い事	*lessons (in piano, judo, etc.)*

JUNIOR HIGH, HIGH SCHOOL

chūgakkō	中学校	*junior high*
kōtōgakkō/kōkō	高等学校・高校	*high school*
bukatsu	部活	*club activities*
juku	塾	*private tutoring school offering classes*
juken	受験	*taking entrance exams*
nyūgaku shiken	入学試験	*school entrance exams*
suberidome	滑り止め	*back-up choice of school*
tōkō kyohi	登校拒否	*refusing to go to school*
ijime	いじめ	*bullying*
kōnai bōryoku	構内暴力	*school violence*
kōkō chūtai	高校中退	*dropping out of high school*
sotsugyōshiki	卒業式	*graduation ceremony*
rōnin	浪人	*"masterless samurai", a student who spends a year at cramming school between high school and university*

Chapter 10 Officialdom

Officialdom

Akira kurosawa's film *Ikiru* shows a frustrated member of the public being passed from pillar to post, directed in ever increasing circles around a government office. Things have changed a great deal since then. Nonetheless, the formalities can still be time-consuming, requiring that you fill out a great deal of paperwork then wait a long time for it to be processed. Know the system, and cooperate without making a fuss: this is generally the quickest way to get what you want. And all officials are sympathetic towards those who can speak, and better still, read the language.

If you come to Japan to work, you will have got a visa from the embassy in your country and a landing permit at the airport. Next stop is the city or ward office. You need to get a "certificate of alien registration" (take your passport and two photos). The card is usually valid for five years and should be carried at all times.

During your stay in Japan, you might be asked to produce a document showing proof of residence. This document is obtained from the same department. You are also required, as are all Japanese nationals, to report any change of address.

Incidentally, the Japanese have to register births, marriages, divorces and deaths in what is known as their family register (**koseki**). Copies of this document are required as proof of identity for certain procedures such as applying for licenses and enrolling in schools. Depending on the situation, you get a copy of the register for the whole family, or the entry for one member of the family.

The same section of the city or ward office deals with registration of name stamps (**jitsuin**), used instead of a signature on legal documents--for example when buying a car, or land, or getting married. A signature is acceptable in such cases but you may be asked to verify your signature; you'll need to get a certificate from your embassy (**sain shōmeisho**). A name stamp used at a bank (**todoke-in**) does not have to be registered, but make sure you use the same stamp for all transactions at that one bank. Any stamp (**mitome-in**) can be used for such mundane transactions as receiving parcels. Name stamps should be looked after with the utmost care and should never be loaned to anyone; people have had their homes signed away as collateral for fraudulent loans.

Your most serious bouts with Japanese officialdom will probably be at Immigration. When you need your visa renewed, check on the internet or telephone beforehand to find out what documents you need and be prepared to fill in lots of forms and wait in line. If you suddenly discover that your visa has expired, go immediately to Immigration (even if you haven't got the papers together), apologize and give a good reason for overstaying. In the dialogue later in this chapter the immigration official overlooks the matter, but you may not be so lucky: it is a serious offence and you could be served a deportation order and be banned from entering the country for five years.

Before you come to live in Japan you should find out whether your country has any reciprocal agreements regarding health and pensions. If none of these apply you will need to pay contributions to Japan's social security plan. If you are employed, you will automatically be enrolled in health and pension insurance plans (**kenkō hoken** and **kōsei nenkin hoken**, respectively) and have the contributions deducted from your pay. If you are self-employed, a student or not working, go to your local government office and enquire about joining the national health insurance plan (**kokumin kenkō hoken**) and pension (**kokumin nenkin**). Incidentally, you are entitled to a lump sum repayment on your pension contributions when you leave Japan.

A word about tax: the Japanese tax year for individuals runs from January to December and the return has to be filed by March 15th. In the run up to the deadline the tax office organizes sessions where you can file your return online. A key document here is the "certificate of tax deducted at source" (**gensen chōshū-hyō**) which your employer will give you in December. And brace yourself for local tax which will be deducted from your pay from June, the amount reflecting your income for the previous year.

To drive in Japan you can use an international driving license, take your overseas license to the licensing center for your area and obtain a Japanese license, or you can take the driving test in Japan. A Japanese license is valid for three years and runs out on your birthday. When you drive, keep to the frustratingly low speed limits and take care not to park illegally: street parking is not allowed. If you're going to buy a car, you'll need a document, which can be obtained from the police, verifying that you have a parking space.

Finally, never drink and drive in Japan. The "legal limit" is extremely low. A whiff of alcohol on the breath will result in heavy fines, not only for the driver but for the others in the car and for the establishment that served the drinks. Get a taxi, or phone for a driving service (**daikō**) to drive both you and your car home safely.

10.01 Extending Your Visa

Before you go to Immigration to extend your visa, check on the internet or telephone to find out what documents you need.

OFFICIAL:

Nyūkoku kanri jimusho.
入国管理事務所。
Immigration Office.

MAX:

Moshi-moshi. Eikaiwa no kyōshi o shite iru Igirisujin desu ga, biza no kōshin ni dō iu shorui ga hitsuyō desu ka?
もしもし。英会話の教師をしているイギリス人ですが、ビザの更新にどういう書類が必要ですか。
Hello. I'm a British teacher of English conversation. What documents do I need to renew my visa?

OFFICIAL:

Gakkō ga hoshōnin to natte iru no desu ka?
学校が保証人となっているのですか。
Is the school your sponsor?

MAX:

Sō desu. Gakkō no rijichō desu.
そうです。学校の理事長です。
Yes. The director of the school.

OFFICIAL:

Sore de wa desu ne, riji-chō ga kaita hoshōsho to gensen chōshūhyō, soshite keiyakusho, sore kara anata no gaikokujin tōroku shōmeisho to pasupōto o motte kite kudasai.
それではですね、理事長が書いた保証書と源泉徴収票、そして契約書、それからあなたの外国人登録証明書とパスポートを持ってきてください。

Then you will need a letter of guarantee from the director, his certificate of tax withheld, and your work contract. Also, please bring your alien registration card and passport.

MAX:

Hai. Arigatō gozaimashita.
はい。ありがとうございました。
I see. Thank you.

10.02 Forgetting to Renew Your Visa

If you have committed this cardinal sin, go straight to Immigration and explain.

LIN:

Sumimasen. Biza ga kiremashita. Ima kara kōshin no tetsu-zuki wa dekimasu ka.
すみません。ビザが切れました。今から更新の手続きはできますか。
Excuse me. My visa's expired. Can I go through the renewal procedures now?

OFFICIAL:

Ē! Itsu kireta?
ええ。いつ切れた？
What! When did it expire?

LIN:

Sengetsu no nijū-go-nichi desu.
先月の25日です。
The twenty-fifth of last month.

OFFICIAL:

Naze konakatta no? Kireta mama da to taiho sareta ka mo shiremasen yo.

なぜ来なかったの。切れたままだと逮捕されたかもしれませんよ。

Why didn't you come? With an expired visa you could have been arrested.

LIN:

Mōshi-wake arimasen. Infuruenza ni kakatte, isshūkan ne-konde shimattan' desu yo. Hontō ni sumimasen deshita.

申し訳ありません。インフルエンザにかかって、1週間寝込んでしまったんですよ。本当にすみませんでした。

I'm very sorry. I caught the flu and was in bed for a week. I'm truly sorry.

OFFICIAL:

Ki ga tsuite sassoku koko ni kita kara, mada yokatta desu yo. Sore de wa, kono shorui o kaite kudasai.

気が付いて早速ここに来たから、まだよかったですよ。それでは、この書類を書いてください。

It's a good thing you came here as soon as you realized. Well, fill in these forms, please.

LIN:

Hai. Wakarimshita.

はい。分かりまました。

All right. Thank you very much.

10.03 Obtaining a Re-entry Permit

Most people get their re-entry permits the same time that they get or renew their work visas. The procedure is simple and usually not time-consuming. Emily is at the airport about to set off for their summer vacation in the States:

OFFICIAL:

Sai-nyūkoku kyoka ga kono pasupōto ni wa arimasen yo!
再入国許可がこのパスポートにはありませんよ。
There's no re-entry permit in this passport!

EMILY:

A, wasurete shimatta !
ア、忘れてしまった！
Oh, no! I forgot!

OFFICIAL: (leading Emily and the children to the airport immigration office)

Chotto kochira e dozō. Nihon o deru no wa hajimete ja nai deshō?
ちょっとこちらへどうぞ。日本を出るのははじめてじゃないでしょう。
Come this way, please. This is not the first time you've left Japan, is it?

EMILY:

Ē. Sō desu.
ええ。そうです。
No, it isn't. (lit. *Yes, that's correct.*)

OFFICIAL:

Naze kyoka o toranakatta desu ka?
なぜ許可をとらなかったですか。
Why didn't you get a permit?

EMILY:

Shigoto ga isogashikute, sono ue ryokō no junbi de, ukkari shite shimaimashita.

仕事が忙しくて、その上、旅行の準備で、うっかりしてしまいました。

I was so busy at work and getting ready for the trip that it slipped my mind.

OFFICIAL:

Mata Nihon ni kaette kuru tsumori deshō?

また、日本へ帰ってくるつもりでしょう。

You plan on coming back to Japan, don't you?

EMILY:

Ē.

ええ。

Yes.

OFFICIAL:

Sai-nyūkoku kyoka ga nai to, saisho kara suteppu o funde, ima no san-nen no biza ga moraerun' desu. Sai-nyūkoku kyoka o wasureru to, ato de anata ga taihen desu yo.

再入国許可がないと、最初からステップを踏んで、今の３年のビザがもらえるんです。再入国許可を忘れると、後であなたがたいへんですよ。

Without a re-entry permit, you'll have to start from step one and work back up to your three-year visa. If you forget your re-entry permit, it's tough on you later on.

EMILY:

Sō desu ne. Kono baai dō shitara ii deshō ka?

そうですね。この場合、どうしたらいいでしょうか

I see. What should I do now?

OFFICIAL:

Konkai ni kagiri koko de oshite agemasu.
今回に限りここで押してあげます。
Just this time, I'll stamp (your passport) here.

EMILY:

Yokatta. Tasukarimashita. Arigatō.
よかった。助かりました。ありがとう。
Thank goodness. That's a great help. Thank you.

OFFICIAL:

Kore kara wasurenaide kudasai.
これから忘れないでください。
Please don't forget again.

EMILY:

Hai. Arigatō gozaimashita.
はい。ありがとうございました。
No, I won't. Thank you very much.

10.04   Losing Your Registration Card

If you lose your alien registration card, you are required to contact your city or ward office within fourteen days.

KATE:

Sumimasen ga, gaijin tōrokusho o nakushite shimaimashita.
すみませんが、外人登録書をなくしてしまいました。
Excuse me, but I've lost my alien registration card.

OFFICIAL:

Itsu desu ka?

いつですか。

When did you lose it?

KATE:

Ototoi. Saifu goto nusumaremashita.

おとい。財布ごと盗まれました。

The day before yesterday, I had my purse and everything in it stolen.

OFFICIAL:

Shashin to pasupōto o motte kimashita ka?

写真とパスポートを持ってきましたか。

Have you brought photographs and your passport?

KATE:

Hai. Shashin ni-mai desu ne.

はい、写真二枚ですね。

Yes. Two photographs.

OFFICIAL:

Sore de wa, koko ni namae, jūsho, nakushita hi to jōkyō o kaite kudasai.

それでは、ここに名前、住所、失くした日と状況を書いてください。

OK. Then please write your name, address, and when and how you lost it here.

Getting Stopped for Speeding

If you are pulled over for speeding, should you pretend that you don't speak Japanese? Be warned. Some policemen speak good English. If you know you are in the wrong, it is probably wise to apologize and to bow as best you can from behind the steering wheel!

POLICEMAN:

Menkyoshō o misete kudasai. Gaikoku-jin tōroku shōmeisho mo dōzo. Sakki rokujū-san-kiro dashite imashita ne.
免許証を見せてください。外国人登録証明書もどうぞ。さっき、63キロ出していましたね。
Show me your driver's license, please. And your alien registration card. You were doing sixty-three kilometers per hour just now.

MAX:

Sō desu ka? Tsui.
そうですか。つい、
Was I? I didn't realize.

POLICEMAN: (looking at license)

O-namae to go-jūsho wa kore de ii desu ne.
お名前とご住所はこれでいいですか。
The name and address on this are correct, aren't they?

MAX:

Hai.
はい。
Yes.

POLICEMAN:

Yōshi ga todokimasu no de, bakkin o harai-konde kudasai. Ihan tensū wa ni-ten ni narimasu. Sankagetsu inai ni ihan ga na-kereba, shizen ni kiemasu kara. Kore kara ki o tsukete kudasai.

用紙が届きますので、罰金を払いこんでください。違反点数は2点になります。3ヶ月以内に違反がなければ、自然に消えますから。これから気をつけてください。

We will send you a form for paying the fine. You will be given two points for the offense, but if you have no offenses in the next three months, the points will be taken off. Please be careful from now on.

10.06 Words and Expressions

CITY AND WARD OFFICES

yakusho	役所	government office
kuyakusho	区役所	ward office
shiyakusho	市役所	city office
Hōmushō	法務省	Ministry of Justice
kōmuin	公務員	government worker
jichitai	自治体	local government
koseki	戸籍	family register
koseki tōhon	戸籍謄本	copy of the whole register
koseki shōhon	戸籍抄本	copy of the entry for one person
gaikokujin tōroku shōmeisho	外国人登録証明書	alien registration card

tōroku-zumi shōmeisho	登録済み証明書	*certificate of residence (for foreigners)*
jūminhyō	住民票	*certificate of residence (for Japanese nationals)*
hanko/inkan	はんこ・印鑑	*name stamp*
inkan tōroku shōmeisho	印鑑登録証明書	*registration certificate for name stamp*

IMMIGRATION

nyūkoku kanri jimusho	入国管理事務所	*Immigration Office*
pasupōto/ryoken	パスポート・旅券	*passport*
biza (zairyū kikan) no kōshin	ビザ（在留期間）の更新	*visa renewal*
zairyū shikaku	在留資格	*residential status*
hoshōnin	保証人	*sponsor*
sainyūkoku	再入国	*re-entry*
sūji sainyūkoku kyoka	数時再入国許可	*multiple re-entry permit*

TAX AND INSURANCE

zeikin	税金	*taxes*
shotokuzei	所得税	*income tax*
jūminzei	住民税	*local tax*
kakutei shinkoku o suru	確定申告をする	*to file a tax return*
gensen chōshū hyō	源泉徴収票	*certificate from employer showing amount of tax deducted at source*

kenkō hoken	健康保険	health insurance (for those employed)
kōsei nenkin hoken	厚生年金保険	welfare pension insurance (for those employed)
kokumin kenkō hoken	国民健康保険	health insurance (for self employed and students)
kokumin nenkin	国民年金	pension insurance (for self employed and students)

POLICE AND DRIVING

keisatsu	警察	police
keisatsusho	警察省	police station
keikan	警官	policeman
shirobai	白バイ	police motorcycle
patokā	パトカー	patrol car
ōtobai	オートバイ	motorcycle
gentsuki	原付き	motorcycle under 50cc, moped
unten menkyoshō	運転免許証	driver's license
unten menkyo o kōshin suru	運転免許を更新する	to renew a driver's license
chūsha ihan	駐車違反	parking offense
supiido ihan	スピード違反	speeding offense
inshu unten	飲酒運転	drunken driving
ketsueki kensa	血液検査	blood test
menkyo teishi	免許停止	suspension of license

menkyo torikeshi	免許取り消し	*disqualification from driving*
nezumi-tori	ネズミとり	*radar trap*
anzen unten	安全運転	*safe driving*
daikō	代行	*driving service*

Chapter 11 Gifts

Gifts

When guests arrive at a wedding reception, they present money wrapped in beautifully decorated envelopes, and receive a present when they leave. Travelers return from weekend trips with boxes of locally made cakes for their friends, relatives, and colleagues and, when they've been abroad, arrive at the airport weighed down with bags of presents. If you give a present to a Japanese friend who's had a baby, you may be surprised to receive a small gift in return a few weeks later. If you go to visit a client, your Japanese colleague may decide to take a small gift of confectionery. When you visit someone's home, you might be pressed with fruit, cakes, and even some of the meal's leftovers to take home. Foreign visitors in particular are often presented with beautiful and expensive gifts, and it's hard to know how to reciprocate.

The protocol and customs regarding gifts are often a cause of anguish for the Japanese themselves, so it's difficult for the foreigner to navigate in this area. Much will depend on the occasion, your relationship with the person concerned, and how long you have lived in the country.

It might help to remember that these customs developed in an earlier age of relative poverty when people in the community would help each other out, chipping in to help finance major life events, such as weddings and funerals, and sharing in times of plenty. Although the outgoings can seem costly, if you are in the cycle, things even out over time. The system of course doesn't travel well outside Japan. Older people in particular may stick with these customs and give generous gifts of money at major life events, even if you are a foreigner and unable to reciprocate over the long term.

Gift giving is not a subject to be taken lightly, and you should consult your Japanese friends to work out a good solution, ideally one that will avoid causing offense but equally will keep you from being drawn into long-term obligations. If you are living in Japan you should probably abide by the rules when attending occasions such as weddings and funerals—after all, your contribution helps fund the event and you will receive a present in return. Find out from others who are going how much money you should take. It may appear churlish not to pay your share, even though customs may be different in your country.

Giving gifts is only half the story. According to Japanese etiquette, the recipient should give a return gift (**o-kaeshi**) equivalent to a third or a half of the value of the original gift. Thus, the new mother sends a gift, traditionally made of sugar, to all those who gave presents for her baby. People who have been ill send **o-kaeshi** to all the people who visited and brought gifts while they were sick. Likewise, the bride and groom arrange for their guests to be given gifts at the end of the wedding reception; these gifts are in fact **o-kaeshi** to the money that the guests presented when they arrived.

But there is an area of the gift-giving scene which foreigners should be wary of. Twice a year, in July and December, people send gifts to underline relationships: companies send gifts to clients to show that they are valued customers and a typical household might send gifts to a special teacher or tutor, the go-between at a wedding, or a family friend who used his or her influence to help find employment. Some people are given gifts because they have recently done or will do something for the family, and others are permanently on the gift list because the family values the relationships.

These two seasons coincide with the twice-yearly bonuses and are important business for the department stores. Gifts range in price from 2,000 to over 20,000 yen. Practical items like ham, soap, salad oil, canned goods and towels make traditional gifts but luxury products are also popular. Once you start giving these gifts you really will be in the cycle.

As a side note, the Japanese do not feel obliged to give gifts at Christmas, something that contrasts with what often happens in the West. In Japan, Christmas gifts are associated with romance and true affection, and, as of yet, there do not seem to be any hard and fast rules.

The milestones of life are also times when people give gifts. Birth, starting primary school, graduating from high school and university, building a house, and the sixtieth birthday are all occasions that are celebrated with gifts. In most instances, gifts are wrapped with special paper marked with the occasion and the donor's name. If you decide to buy a gift for such an occasion, bear in mind that prestige is attached to where the gift is bought; so the same gift is better wrapped in the paper of one department store rather than another. Make sure you tell the sales assistant that the purchase is a gift and get it wrapped appropriately, and despatched.

Money is often given on occasions like passing school entrance examinations, graduation, marriage, and sickness. The money is always cash, preferably new bills, and is put in special envelopes which are on sale everywhere.

As we have seen, gift giving in Japan is complex, stylized and based on long-standing relationships. Due to the short-term nature of most visitors' connections with Japan, you are not expected to reciprocate. Nonetheless you might want to take the time later to choose something special from your own country. Wine, china, ornaments, leather goods, CDs, a favorite brandy or whisky—these all make gifts that please.

Having Something Gift-wrapped

Gifts for formal occasions used to be wrapped with a heavy white paper and tied with stiff red and white strings. Nowadays this motif is printed on a special paper (**noshi** のし) and store assistants, after neatly wrapping your gift in the store's paper, will ask if you want this added.

KIM:

Sumimasen. Kono urushi no o-bon, kudasai.
すみません。このうるしのお盆ください。
Excuse me. I'd like this lacquer tray, please.

SHOP ASSISTANT:

Hai. O-tsukaimono desu ka?
はい。おつかいものですか。
Thank you. Is it a gift?

KIM:

Hai. Kekkon-iwai desu kara, tsutsunde kudasai.
はい。結婚祝いですから、包んでください。
Yes. It's a wedding present so please wrap it (appropriately).

SHOP ASSISTANT:

Noshi o tsukemasu ka?
のしを付けますか。
Shall I put the formal gift paper on it?

KIM:

Iie. Kekkō desu. Kawari ni ribon o tsukete kudasai.
いいえ。結構です。代わりにリボンをつけてください。
No, thank you. Please put a ribbon on it instead.

SHOP ASSISTANT:

Hai, kashikomarimashita.
はい。かしこまりました。
Certainly, madam.

11.02 Offering a Gift

In formal situations, gifts are usually presented after everyone has been seated. When offering a gift wrapped in formal paper, present it with both hands and make sure that the writing on the paper is right side up as it faces the recipient. Japanese often belittle the gifts they offer with phrases like:

- **Tsumaranai mono desu ga.**
  つまらないものですが。
  This is a trifling thing.

- **Honno wazuka desu ga.**
  ほんのわずかですが。
  It is only a small amount.

- **Kokoro-bakari no mono desu ga.**
  心ばかりのものですが。
  It's only a small token.

In business, gifts are offered, rather inconspicuously, just before leaving:

- **Honno o-shirushi desu ga.**
  ほんのお印しですが。
  This is just a small token (of our relationship).

In less formal situations, you might prefer to use one of the follow-ing:

- **Sukoshi desu ga, dōzo.**
  少しですが、どうぞ。
  This is just a very small token, but please (go ahead and take it).

- **Tai no o-kashi desu. Dōzo, meshiagatte kudasai.**
  タイのお菓子です。どうぞ、召し上がってください。
  This is some candy from Thailand. I hope you like it. (lit. *Please eat it.*)

- **Kanada no shashin-shū desu. Dōzo, goran kudasai.**
  カナダの写真集です。どうぞ、ご覧ください。
  This is a book of photographs of Canada. I hope you enjoy look-ing at it. (lit. *Please look at it.*)

- **Tezukuri no kukkii desu ga, dōzo tabete mite kudasai.**
  手作りのクッキーですが、どうぞ、食べてみてください。
  I made these cookies myself. I hope you like them. (lit. *Please try them.*)

- **Nani ga ii ka to mayoimashita ga, yōshu ga o-suki da to kiki-mashita no de, kore o motte mairimashita. Kitto ki ni itte itadakeru to omoimasu.**
  なにがいいかと迷いましたが、洋酒がお好きだと聞きまし
  たので、これを持ってまいりました。きっと、気に入ってい
  ただけると思います。
  I didn't know what to give you but then I heard that you like West-ern liquors. So, this is what I brought. I'm sure you'll like it.

Opening a Gift

Japanese don't usually open gifts right taway. (You don't see this so much these days but the gift may first be put on the family altar for a while.) If you would like the recipient to open the gift, say:

- **Akete mite kudasai. Ki ni itte itadakeru to iin' desu ga.**
  開けてみてください。気に入っていただけるといいんですが。
  Please open it. I do hope you like it.

- **Akete mo ii desu ka?**
  開けてもいいですか。
  May I open it?

11.04

Expressing Thanks for a Gift

Show your appreciation like this:

- **Subarashii!**
  すばらしい！
  Wonderful!

- **Kirei desu ne!**
  きれいですね。
  It's really pretty!

- **Oishisō!**
  おいしそう！
  It looks delicious!

- **Wā, ureshii!**
  わあ、うれしい！
  Ah, great! (used mostly by women)

- **Dōmo arigatō. Daikōbutsu desu.**
  どうもありがとう。大好物です。
  Thank you. I'm very fond of this (usually referring to food).

- **Ii kinen ni narimasu.**
  いい記念になります。
  It will be a good souvenir.

- **Kanai mo yorokobimasu.**
  かないも喜びます。
  My wife will love it too.

- **Kyōshuku desu.**
  恐縮です。
  I am truly grateful.

In formal situations you may want to use the traditional phrase for receiving gifts:

> • **Kore wa go-teinei ni arigatō gozaimashita.**
> これはご丁寧にありがとうございました。
> *How very kind of you. Thank you very much.*

The next time you talk to someone who gave you a gift, don't forget to thank them again:

> • **Senjitsu wa dōmo arigatō gozaimashita.**
> 先日はどうもありがとうございました。
> *Thank you for (your gift) the other day.*
>
> • **Konaida wa dōmo gochisō-sama deshita. Taihen oishikatta desu.**
> こないだはどうもごちそうさまでした。たいへんおいしかったです。
> *Thank you for (your delicious gift) the other day. It was very good.*

11.05 Gift Suggestions

Here are some ideas for gifts for different occasions.

VISITING PEOPLE FOR DINNER:
  Flowers, fruit, wine.

VISITING SOMEONE TO MAKE A REQUEST:
  Small box of cakes or candies.

VISITING AN IMPORTANT CLIENT:
  High quality confectionery, book, or some practical item of high quality and good design. Something from your home country would be best.

VISITING FRIENDS:

Something homemade.

SUMMER GIFTS:

Towel, soap, tea, iced tea or coffee set, fruit juice, beer, dried noodles, fruit, potted plant. These are gifts associated with coolness.

YEAR END GIFTS:

Wine, whisky, ham, sausage, cheese, chocolates, cyclamen plant. These are gifts that can be used over the Christmas and New Year holidays.

VISITING THE SICK:

Money, book, CD. (No rooted plants.)

AN EXHIBITION OR CONCERT:

Money, flowers, box of cakes or candies.

11.06 Telephoning to Say Thank You

Gifts should be acknowledged right away. A formal postcard (*see* page 297) is the proper way to express thanks but a brief phone call will often suffice.

> EMILY:
>
> **Tērā desu ga, kyō wa o-todokemono o itadakimashite, arigatō gozaimashita.**
>
> テーラーですが、今日はお届け物をいただきまして、ありが
> とうございました。
>
> *This is Mrs. Taylor. Your gift arrived today. Thank you very much.*

MRS SUZUKI:

Iie, honno kokoro-bakari no mono desu.

いいえ、ほんの心ばかりのものです。

It's only a small token.

EMILY:

Chōdo hoshikatta mono desu. Arigatō gozaimashita. Mina-sama o-genki desu ka?

ちょうどほしかったものです。ありがとうございました。皆さま、お元気ですか。

It was just what I wanted. Thank you very much. Is everyone fine?

MRS SUZUKI:

Hai. Okage-sama de. Aikawarazu bata bata shite imasu ga.

はい、お陰様で。相変わらず、バタバタしていますが、

Yes, thank you. Rushing around as usual.

EMILY:

Chikai uchi ni mata o-ai shimashō ne.

近いうちにまたお会いしましょうね。

Let's get together soon.

MRS SUZUKI:

Sō shimashō. Waza-waza o-denwa arigatō gozaimashita.

そうしましょう。わざわざお電話ありがとうございました。

Yes, let's do. Thank you for calling.

EMILY:

Iie. Sore de wa, shitsurei itashimasu.

いいえ、それでは、失礼いたします。

Not at all. Goodbye.

Gift Papers and Money Envelopes

Here are some of the phrases written or printed on gift papers and envelopes:

o-rei	御礼	*gift or fee for a service* (lit. *thanks*)
kotobuki	寿	*gift for a wedding or other felicitous occasion*
o-iwai	お祝い	*gift for a wedding or other felicitous occasion*
uchi-iwai	内祝い	*return gift (wedding or other felicitous occasion)*
o-senbetsu	お餞別	*gift for someone who is going away*
kinen-hin	記念品	*gift to mark an occasion or achievement*
o-mimai	お見舞い	*gift or money for someone who is ill*
kaiki-iwai	快気祝い	*return gift to above*
o-toshidama	お年玉	*money given at New Year to children*
o-tanjō iwai	お誕生祝い	*gift to a new-born baby; also for a birthday*
go-nyūgaku iwai	ご入学祝い	*gift or money on entering elementary school, junior high, high school, or college*
go-sotsugyō iwai	ご卒業祝い	*gift or money on graduation*
go-reizen	ご霊前	*money given at funerals*
go-butsuzen	ご仏前	*money given at a Buddhist funeral service held forty-nine days after a death*

Words and Expressions

11.08

okurimono	贈もの	*gift, often a small present such as a birthday gift*
o-chūgen	お中元	*summer gift*
o-seibo	お歳暮	*year-end gift*
gifuto	ギフト	*gift, usually an o-chūgen or o-seibo gift*
purezento	プレゼント	*present, free gift*
miyage	土産	*gift brought back from a trip, souvenir*
te-miyage	手土産	*small gift taken when making a visit (business)*
shōhinken	商品券	*gift vouchers*
o-kaeshi	お返し	*return gift*
kanreki	還暦	*60th birthday*
noshi(-gami)	のし（紙）	*formal gift paper*
kane o tsutsumu	金を包む	*wrapping money (in an envelope), or the act of giving money*

Chapter 12 Weddings

Weddings

If you're invited to a wedding, you'll probably not witness the ceremony itself, which is generally a private affair involving only the two families. (Sometimes the couple will have been officially married months before, since all that's required is that both parties submit the paperwork and register the marriage **(seki o ireru)**. Your invitation will be for the reception, or **hirōen**, which means "announcement." It's a formal announcement to society that the marriage has taken place. It's not uncommon to have several receptions. If the two families live far apart, for example, receptions will be held in both communities.

In earlier times, the two families gathered at the bridegroom's home to wait for the bride, who would arrive hours behind schedule. The lively celebrations that followed the simple, private wedding ceremony went on late into the night and the festivities continued for days, during which several receptions were held to introduce the new couple to the various groups in the community.

The marriage ceremony today usually takes place an hour or so before the reception in a small Shinto shrine or Christian-style chapel within the hotel or wedding hall. In a Shinto wedding, the ceremony begins with the priest waving his staff of white paper strands over the assembly as he invokes the gods with prayers. After the couple exchange wedding rings, the groom reads a pledge that is similar to the vows of a Christian marriage. To solemnize the marriage, the couple sip saké from a set of three flat cups. Christian weddings, performed with the traditional vows and hymns, are also popular although, in most cases, the bride and groom have no connection with any particular church or religion.

As mentioned earlier, giving money at weddings is a custom that started in poorer days when friends and relatives of the two families contributed to lighten the financial burden. The money that guests take to weddings nowadays is meant to cover the cost of the meal and the gift they will receive, and hopefully leave some over. The going rate is 20,000 yen per guest but get advice from Japanese friends who are going. Wrap your contribution to the ceremony in one of the special envelopes beautifully decorated with gold, silver and red macramé.

People do give wedding presents either instead of or as well as money. If you balk at giving money and feel strongly that you want to give a more personal gift, one compromise might be to give a small, personal gift beforehand (get it sent in advance), and after consultation with others attending the wedding, take a modest sum of money to the reception.

Wedding receptions these days are a lot less formal than they used to be, typified by a new trend for "house weddings" where the party will have private use of a guesthouse for a smaller, more personal reception. Nonetheless the ceremony will begin with a formal announcement that the marriage ceremony has been solemnized and brief personal histories of both partners. Then there will be speeches, often by the bosses of the bride and the groom, stressing the reliability of the two partners and hopes for a good marriage or **akarui katei**. These speeches tend to be stiff and formal, and not until the toast, which precedes the feast, does the party begin.

Whatever the venue, the whole proceedings will be highly orchestrated and professional. Not only does the meal have many courses of the best cuisine, but the two stars of the show make dramatic entrances, changing costumes once or twice within the span of a few hours. The cutting of the cake and the multi-media presentations are all well done. It's an experience not be missed.

Replying to an Invitation

A reply card is usually sent with the invitation. Fill in your name, address, and whether or not you will attend. Cross out the respectful prefix **go** since you are referring to yourself. You can also add a few words of congratulation or, in the case of a refusal, a short explanation and apology.

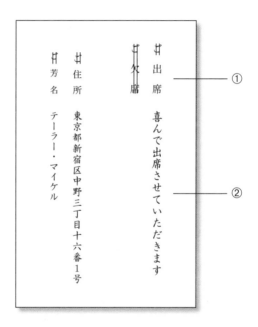

御出席
御欠席

喜んで出席させていただきます

御住所　東京都新宿区中野三丁目十六番1号

御芳名　テーラー・マイケル

① ②

Accepting an Invitation

① ②

Shusseki: Yorokonde shusseki sasete itadakimasu.
Will attend: I look forward to attending.

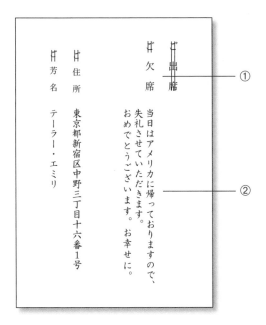

ご出席

欠席 ①

当日はアメリカに帰っておりますので、
失礼させていただきます。
おめでとうございます。お幸せに。 ②

住所　東京都新宿区中野三丁目十六番1号

芳名　テーラー・エミリ

Declining an Invitation

Kesseki: Tōjitsu wa Amerika ni kaette orimasu no de shitsurei sasete itadakimasu. Omedetō gozaimasu. O-shiawase ni.

Will not attend: I will be back in the United States that day and regret that I will not be able to attend. Congratulations. I wish you much happiness.

12.02 Arriving at the Reception

On the day of the reception, dress in your finery; **heifuku** (平服 which means "everyday clothes") on an invitation should not be taken literally. Because there are preliminaries to be completed, arrive at the venue about fifteen minutes before the announced time. At the reception desk, present your money in its special envelope and sign the guest book. If you have sent a gift instead of giving money, explain the situation to the people at the desk:

- **O-iwai o okurimashita no de.**
  お祝いを贈りましたので。
  I have already sent a gift.

As you enter the banquet room, greet the bride and groom and both sets of parents who will all be waiting at the entrance. Bow or shake hands and offer your congratulations to all concerned:

- **Omedetō gozaimasu.**
  おめでとうございます。
  Congratulations.

You could compliment the bride:

- **O-kirei desu ne.**
  おきれいですね。
  You look lovely.

12.03   Leaving the Reception

The same group will see you out as you leave. It is then appropriate to wish the bride and groom every happiness:

- **O-shiawase ni.**
  お幸せに。
  I wish you every happiness.

You can also thank and/or compliment the parents:

- **Subarashii hirōen deshita.**
  すばらしい披露宴でした。
  It was a wonderful reception.

12.04 Wedding Speeches

The formal atmosphere at the beginning of a Japanese wedding reception can be unnerving to anyone who has to make a speech. Remember that the first few speeches are ceremonial. If you are the boss of the bride or the groom, you may well be one of the first to speak. If so, your speech must be very well prepared.

Comments alluding to marriage as being one foot in the grave and jokes of that ilk are out of place at this stage of a Japanese wedding. The whole tone must be felicitous. It is customary to eulogize the bride and groom as paragons of beauty, talent, and intelligence. Check your speech too for taboo words (*see* p. 246).

A toast comes after the last main speech, and this is followed by more frank and amusing speeches given by friends of the bride and groom. Some incident that throws light on the bride or groom's personality, or some explanation of how they met provides a welcome contrast to the polite clichés that characterize the formal speeches before the toast.

Foreigners are frequently invited to Japanese weddings and asked to give speeches even though they may have only a casual acquaintance with the bride or the groom; the intention is often to give the wedding an "international" flavor. If you are giving a speech, start with some conventional words of congratulation and speak slower than usual so the audience can adjust to the fact that you are speaking Japanese. Although jokes should be used with discretion, a few phrases or epigrams in English often prove popular. You can even opt out of speaking Japanese altogether and sing a song instead. Do not dismiss this out of hand as the audience will certainly enjoy it and there may well be singing later on in the proceedings.

12.05 Giving a Formal Speech

This speech, suitable if you are a main guest, shows the kind of sentiments one is expected to express and the kind of language to use. After a few words of congratulation the speaker, who is the bride's boss, introduces himself and praises the bride's personality and accomplishments. Although he finishes with a play on words, he is careful to maintain a formal tone throughout the speech.

Takuya-san, Yumi-san, soshite go-ryōke no minasama, omedetō gozaimasu.

Kokoro kara o-yorokobi o mōshi-agemasu.

Watakushi wa shinpu no tsutomete oraremasu Ekoshisutemu no Nihon manējā no Tērā de gozaimasu. Honjitsu wa o-maneki itadakimashite, kōei ni zonjimasu.

Yumi-san wa watakushidomo no kaisha ni haitte sannen ni narimasu ga, tonikaku akaruku, shokuba no mūdo mēkā desu. Mochiron shigoto no men de mo sekkyokuteki de, eigyō shien ya kokyaku taiō de, iwaba kaisha no saizensen to mo ieru bunya de katsuyaku shite irasshaimasu. Kore kara mo sono chikara o ōi ni kitai shite orimasu.

Kyō, Yumi-san no utsukushii hana-yome sugata o haiken itashimashite, kangeki shite orimasu.

Shigoto to katei no ryōritsu wa dono kuni de mo kantan na mono de wa arimasen.

Takuya-san to Yumi-san wa chikara o awasete, jikan o yūkō ni katsuyō shite, enman na katei o kizuite itadakitai mono desu.

Kongo mo Yumi-san wa shain no yoki senpai to shite, shigoto to katei no baransu o umaku totte ganbatte hoshii, mata sapōto shite ikitai to kangaete imasu.

Saigo ni, kekkon wa chōki tōshi de ari, aijō o kotsu-kotsu tsumitatenai to manki ni wa narimasen. Dōka, o-futaritomo "tanki" * o okosanaide, shōrai no ōki na minori o uketotte kudasai.

Kyō wa hontō ni omedetō gozaimasu.

拓也さん、有美さん、そしてご両家のみなさま、おめでとうございます。

心からお喜びを申し上げます。

私は新婦の勤めておられますエコシステムの日本マネジャーのテーラーでございます。本日はお招きいただきまして、光栄に存じます。

有美さんは私どもの会社に入って3年になりますが、とにかく明るく、職場のムードメーカーです。もちろん仕事の面でも積極的で、営業支援や、顧客対応で、いわば会社の最前線とも言える分野で活躍していらっしゃいます。これからも、その力を大いに期待しております。

きょう、有美さんの美しい花嫁姿を拝見いたしまして、感激しております。

仕事と家庭の両立はどの国でも簡単なものではありません 。

拓也さんと有美さんは、力を合わせて、時間を有効に活用して、円満な家庭を築いていただきたいものです。今後も、有美さんは社員のよき先輩として、仕事と家庭のバランスをうまくとって、がんばってほしい、またサポートしていきたいと考えています。

最後に、結婚は長期投資であり、愛情をこつこつ積み立てないと満期にはなりません。どうか、お二人とも「短期」*を起こさないで、将来の大きな実を受け取ってください。

今日は、本当におめでとうございます。

* This is a pun on the word **tanki**, which means both "impatient" (短気) and "short-term" (短期).

Takuya, Yumi, and both families, congratulations. I offer my sincere congratulations.

My name is Taylor and I am the manager of the Japan office of Eco-Systems, where the bride is employed. It is a great honor to be invited here today.

Yumi joined our company three years ago. She's very cheerful, in fact she sets the mood in the office. Of course she's very positive in her work too. She's active at the very forefront of the company in sales support and customer response. I have great hopes of her in the future.

I am very moved today to see Yumi on her wedding day looking so lovely.

Managing both work and a family is not easy in any country. We all want Takuya and Yumi to work together to make best use of their time to build a happy household. I hope Yumi will be a good role model for people in the company in creating a good balance between work and family. And I would like to support her in this.

Finally, marriage is a long-term investment that doesn't reach maturity unless there are regular additional instalments of affection. May you both temper your impatience,* and enjoy the fruits of your investment for many years to come.

As for today, my sincerest congratulations!

12.06

Giving an Informal Speech (1)

This lively, cheerful speech is given by a female friend of the bride.

Yumi-san, Takuya-san, omedetō gozaimasu.
Kyō wa o-maneki itadaki, arigatō gozaimashita.
Watashi wa, Yumi-san no yūjin de, Kimu Yun Hii to iimasu. Kankoku shusshin desu.
Kyō, o-iwai no kotoba o sasete itadakimasu.

Yumi-san wa kappatsu na akarui josei desu. Soshite kyō, go-ran no yō ni utsukushii josei de mo arimasu.

Sore kara, rekishi ga asai no desu ga, o- ryōri wa totemo jōzu desu.

Motomoto amari ryōri ni kanshin o motanai hito deshita ga, rokkagetsu hodo mae desho ka? Ryōri gakkō ni kayou yō ni narimashita. Soshite, ii resutoran o sagashidashi, watashi o sasottari shite, shokuji o shinagara, tanoshiku ryōri no hanashi o suru yō ni narimashita.

Sono henshin ni tsuite, saisho wa yoku rikai dekimasen deshita ga, sūkagetsu mae ni subete ga akiraka ni narimashita. Takuya-san to no majika na kekkon ga sono haikei ni arimashita.

Dōka, futari de oishii o-ryōri o tanoshinde, ii omoide o tsukuri, shiawase na katei o tsukutte kudasai.

Hontō ni kyō wa omedetō gozaimasu. Itsumademo o-shiawase ni.

有美さん、拓也さん、おめでとうございます。
今日は、お招きいただき、ありがとうございました。
私は、有美さんの友人で、金英姫といいます。韓国出身です。
今日、お祝いの言葉をさせていただきます。

有美さんは活発な明るい女性です。そして今日、ご覧のように美しい女性でもあります。

それから、歴史が浅いのですが、お料理はとても上手です。

もともとあまり料理に関心を持たない人でしたが、6ヶ月ほど前でしょうか。料理学校に通うようになりました。そして、いいレストランを探し出し、私を誘ったりして、食事しながら、楽しく料理の話しをするようになりました。

その変身について、最初はよく理解できませんでしたが、数か月前にすべてが明らかになりました。拓也さんとの間近な結婚がその背景にありました。

どうか、二人でおいしいお料理を楽しんで、いい思い出をつくり、幸せな家庭を作ってください。

本当に今日はおめでとうございます。いつまでもお幸せに。

Congratulations, Yumi and Takuya. Thank you for inviting me today. I am a friend of Yumi's and my name is Kim Young Hee. I'm from South Korea.

Today I would like to say a few words of congratulation.

Yumi is a lively and cheerful woman, and as we can see today, also very beautiful.

And, though this is quite recent, she's a very good cook.

She was never very interested in food but, was it about six months ago? She started to go to cookery school. And she would search out good restaurants, invite me along, and whilst we were eating she would enjoy talking about cooking.

At first I couldn't understand this change in her, but then a few months ago all was revealed. Her impending marriage to Takuya was the reason behind this.

May you both enjoy good cooking, make good memories and build a happy family.

Congratulations to you both today. I wish you every happiness always.

Giving an Informal Speech (2)

Lin gives this speech as a friend of the bridegroom.

Takuya-san, Yumi-san, go-kekkon omedetō. Watashi wa shinro Itō-kun no yūjin no Rin Bun Ho desu. Kyō wa o-maneki itadaki, arigatō gozaimasu. Hajimete Nihon no kekkon-shiki ni shusseki shimasu no de, kore wa subarashii keiken desu.

Sate, toki wa sakunen no shichigatsu. Jitaku no hōmu pātei de, aru wakai otoko ga yūki o motte gaishikei kinmu no kawaii hito ni eigo de iroiro shitsumon shite imasu. Kaiwa wa migoto ni hazumimasu. Nanto subarashii eigo no jōtatsu darō to watashi wa kangeki shimashita. Kono toki no futari ga hoka de mo arimasen. Genzai watashitachi no mae de sakan ni terete iru shinrō-shinpu na no desu. Sono ato watashi wa Chūgoku e modorimashita kara, dō natta no ka yoku shirimasen ga, kare to kanojo wa sono natsu no aida ni o-atsuku natta yō desu.

Tomodachi ni yoreba, kekkon wa atsui o-furo no yō na mono da sō desu. Haitte shimau to, sore-hodo atsui mono de wa arimasen! Shikashi karera wa Nihon no oidaki-buro no koto wa shiranai no desu! Dōka, Takuya, Yumi-san. Nihon-jin no ai no bānā o tsukatte, o-futari no kekkon o itsumademo atsui mono ni shite kudasai. Dōzo, o-shiawase ni.

拓也さん、有美さん、ご結婚おめでとう。私は新朗伊藤君の友人の林文宝です。今日は、お招きいただき、ありがとうございます。はじめて、日本の結婚式に出席しますので、これは素晴しい経験です。

さて、時は昨年の7月。自宅のホームパーテイで、ある若い男が勇気をもって外資系勤務のかわいい人に英語でいろいろ質問しています。会話は見事に弾みます。何と素晴らしい英語の

上達だろうと私は感激しました。この時の二人が他でもありません。現在私たちの前で盛んにてれている新朗、新婦なのです。その後、私は中国へ戻りましたから、どうなったのかよく知りませんが、彼と彼女はその夏の間にお熱くなったようです。

友達によれば、結婚は熱いお風呂のようなものだそうです。入ってしまえば、それほど熱いものではありません。しかし、彼らは日本の追いだき風呂のことは知らないのです。どうか、拓也、有美さん、日本人の愛のバーナーを使って、お二人の結婚をいつまでも熱いものにしてください。どうぞ、お幸せに。

Takuya, Yumi, congratulations on your wedding day! I am a friend of Ito's, the groom, and my name is Lin Wenbao. Thank you very much for inviting me today. This is the first Japanese wedding I have ever attended and it is a wonderful experience.

Let me take you back to July last year. At a party at my house a young man bravely asks a sweet woman who works at a foreign company questions in English. The conversation is wonderfully animated. I marvel at their progress in English. These two were none other than the bride and groom, who are looking extremely embarrassed right now! Soon after that I returned to China and don't really know what happened, but it seems that things really heated up between them during that summer.

My friends tell me that marriage is like a hot bath; it's not so hot once you're in it! But they don't know about the Japanese bath, which can be heated up whenever it cools. Takuya, Yumi, may you use the Japanese burner of love to heat your marriage forever. I wish you every happiness.

Proposing the Toast

The toast marks the end of the ceremonial speeches and the start of the wedding feast. If you wish, add a few words of introduction to the following toast.

Dewa kanpai no ondo o torasete itadakimasu. Takuya-san, Yumi-san, kyō wa omedetō gozaimasu. Sara ni, Itō-ke, Satō-ke no masu-masu no go-han'ei, awasete go-rinseki no minasama no go-kenshō o kinen itashimashite, kanpai o itashimasu! Kanpai!

では、乾杯の音頭をとらせていただきます。拓也さん、有美さん、今日はおめでとうございます。更に、伊藤家、佐藤家のますますのご繁栄、あわせてご臨席の皆様のご健勝を祈念いたしまして、乾杯をいたします。カンパイ！

I would like to propose a toast: To Takuya and Yumi on this happy day. To the prosperity of the Ito and Sato families, and to the good health of us all. Congratulations!

12.09 Taboo Words

The use of certain words, **imi kotoba**, during weddings is believed to be unlucky. This superstition dates from the Heian period, became widespread in the fifteenth century, and survives even today. These words are shunned because of their associations with an unsuccessful marriage. For example, **kiru** (to cut) is not used because of its connotations with **en o kiru** (to break off a relationship); **kyonen** (last year) because it is written with the character meaning to leave; and **kuri-kaesu** (to repeat) because it hints at divorce and remarriage.

Following is a list of common taboo words, and for some of them, appropriate substitutes.

	TABOO WORD	MEANING	SUBSTITUTE WITH
kyonen	去年	last year	昨年 **sakunen**
kaeru	帰る	to leave	中座・失礼する **chūza** or **shitsurei suru**
kiru	切る	to cut	ナイフを入れる **naifu o ireru**
owari	終わり	end, close	お開き **o-hiraki**
saru	去る	to leave	avoid
wakareru	別れる	to part	avoid
modoru	戻る	to return	avoid
yaburu	破る	to break	avoid
kuri-kaesu	繰り返す	to repeat	avoid
akiru	あきる	to become bored	avoid
tabi-tabi	たびたび	again and again	avoid
mō ichido	もう一度	once more	avoid

12.10 Sending a Telegram

If you cannot attend a wedding, you might consider sending a telegram.
Internet sites have hundreds of examples. Here's a selection:

- **Go-kekkon omedetō gozaimasu.**
  ご結婚おめでとうございます。
  Congratulations on your marriage.

- **Go-kekkon o shukushi, sue-nagaku sachi ōkare to inorimasu.**
  ご結婚を祝し、末永く幸多かれと祈ります。
  Congratulations on your marriage, and much happiness always.

- **Omedetō. Suteki na o-futari ni kanpai.**
  おめでとう。すてきなお二人にカンパイ！
  Congratulations. A toast to a wonderful couple!

- **Yorokobi ippai shiawase ippai no ima no kimochi itsumademo.**
  喜びいっぱい幸せいっぱいの今の気持ちいつまでも。
  May the joy and happiness you feel today last forever.

12.11 Epigrams

Here are some epigrams, with translations, just for fun.

- **Kekkon seikatsu wa ōku no kutsū o motsu ga, dokushin sei-katsu wa yorokobi o motanai.**
  結婚生活は多くの苦痛を持つが、独身生活は喜びを持たない。
  Marriage has many pains, but celibacy has few pleasures. (Samuel Johnson)

- **Yoki otto wa yoki tsuma o tsukuru.**
  よき夫はよき妻を作る。
  A good husband makes a good wife. (Robert Burton)

- **Josei wa rikai subeki mono dewa naku, ai subeki mono de aru.**
  女性は理解すべきものではなく、愛すべきものである。
  Women are meant to be loved, not understood. (Oscar Wilde)

- **Kekkon-mae wa ryōme o ake, kekkon shitara katame o tsubure.**
  結婚前は両目を開け、結婚したら片目をつぶれ。
  Keep your eyes wide open before marriage and half-shut afterwards. (Anonymous)

12.12 Words and Expressions

konyaku	婚約	*engagement*
yuinō	結納	*betrothal present or ceremony*
o-yome ni iku	お嫁にいく	*to get married (woman)*
kekkon todoke	結婚届け	*marriage certificate*
seki o ireru	籍を入れる	*to register a marriage*
kekkonshiki	結婚式	*wedding*
shinzen kekkonshiki	神前結婚式	*Shinto wedding*
san-san-ku-do	三三九度	*part of the marriage rite in which the couple exchanges saké cups*
kirisutokyō kekkonshiki	キリスト教結婚式	*Christian wedding*

shinrō/hanamuko	新朗・花婿	*bridegroom*
shinpu/hanayome	新婦・花嫁	*bride*
kekkon hirōen	結婚披露宴	*wedding reception*
kekkon iwai	結婚祝い	*wedding present or money donation*
hikidemono	引き出物	*gift for a guest*
go-ryōke	ご両家	*the two families*
shuhin	主賓	*main guest*
kinen shashin	記念写真	*(wedding) photograph*
o-ironaoshi	お色直し	*bride's change of costume*
shukuji	祝辞	*wedding speech*
shukuden	祝電	*congratulatory telegram*
rikon	離婚	*divorce*

Chapter 13 Funerals

Chapter 13

Funerals

Not so long ago a death was an occasion for the community to come together. Friends and acquaintances who lived nearby would rush to the house to offer condolences, often showing great emotion. Close relatives would take several days off work to help with the funeral arrangements, and children were automatically excused from school for a prescribed number of days. The wives in the neighborhood would take over the kitchen and prepare mainly vegetarian food for the family in mourning and for the many visitors who would come to pay their respects. During this period, the house would be a hive of activity. There is a saying that a grandparent's funeral is a grandchild's festival (**Jiji-baba no sōshiki wa mago no matsuri**).

Today the ceremonies are more likely to be held at a funeral parlor, which will handle all the arrangements. The descriptions in this chapter describe such a funeral. Perhaps the only vestige of the community pitching in to help is the custom of mourners contributing money towards the expenses of the funeral. But even this is giving way to a new trend for smaller, more personal funerals for close friends and family.

Generally speaking, when a person dies in Japan, the body is brought as soon as possible to the house, or to the funeral parlor, and laid out with the head to the north, a direction usually avoided when sleeping. The body is dressed in a white kimono worn right over left instead of the usual left over right, and given a purse containing the fare for the ferry across the Buddhist version of the River Styx (**Sanzu no kawa**), and a walking stick and straw sandals for the arduous journey to paradise. Watch the film Departures (**Okuribito**) for a glimpse of what goes on behind the scenes.

The wake takes place the same day or the next day and is a religious service starting at about six or seven in the evening. The funeral, usually occurring the following day, is a brief, private service held in the home, at a temple, or at a funeral home. In Japan cremation is the norm, and the family returns from the crematory with the urn of ashes and places it on a specially erected altar. Next, a general memorial service is usually held. This can be the same day, or several days or even months later. According to Buddhist practices, mourning lasts for forty-nine days, and sometime during this period the ashes are interred in the family grave.

If the deceased was a close friend or a business acquaintance, you must decide whether to attend the wake, the memorial service, or both. For the memorial service, mourning clothes should be worn. This means black suit and tie for men, and black suit or dress with plain, black shoes and purse for women. Jewelry should not be worn, except for pearls. Unless you have heard that offerings will not be accepted (**go-jitai mōshiagemasu**), you should prepare an offering in a special envelope used for funerals. These are either made out of a stiff white paper folded and tied elegantly with black and silver strings or printed with this design and are sold at stationers and convenience stores. Those marked (**go-reizen**—before the spirit of the departed) are for any funeral regardless of religion, and those marked (**go-butsuzen**—before the Buddha) are for Buddhist memorial services after the forty-ninth day. The amount you give depends on your relationship to the deceased; most people enclose five or ten thousand yen. Check with a friend as the amount depends on your relationship with the deceased and on the region. You will receive a small token gift in return.

When you arrive at the memorial service, present your donation at the reception table and write your name and address in the guest book. Next, turn to the family of the deceased, who will be lined up to receive the mourners. You can bow, shake hands, or express your regret in English or Japanese, anything that comes naturally.

Envelope for offering at a funeral

The room where the service is held will have a photograph of the deceased and, under it, the box containing the urn of ashes, or the coffin. The display will be richly decorated with flowers. The service begins with a religious ceremony lasting for about thirty minutes and is followed by short eulogies addressed to the deceased. After speeches of thanks by the chairman of the funeral committee and by the chief mourner, the general mourners file up to offer either incense or flowers. At Shinto funerals, which are rare, branches of **sakaki** さかき (*Cleyera japonica*) are offered.

Attending funerals is considered very important and most companies' work rules allow staff time off for mourning which is calculated separately from annual paid leave. Also, Japanese frequently attend services for a parent or even a grandparent of an acquaintance, even though they may never have met the deceased. If the deceased was your friend or a business acquaintance with whom you had regular contact, you should at least make an effort to attend the memorial service.

Being Informed of a Death

A mutual acquaintance will probably inform you by telephone that someone has died. You might want to find out what that person intends to do and then ask if you may go along.

KATO:

Kato desu ga. Takahashi-buchō no otōsan ga kyō nakunara-retan' desu yo.

加藤ですが。高橋部長のお父さんが今日亡くなられたんですよ。

This is Kato. Did you hear that Takahashi's father died today?

MICHAEL:

Sore-wa sore-wa.

それはそれは。

I am sorry to hear that.

KATO:

Sore-de, o-tsuya wa kyō no roku-ji-han ni go-jitaku de okonawareru yō da ga, kokubetsu-shiki wa jūyokka no gogo ni-ji ni Dai-ichi Kaikan de okonau yotei da sō desu.

それで、お通夜は今日の6時半にご自宅で行われるようだが、告別式は14日の午後2時に第一会館で行う予定だそうです。

The wake will be held today at 6:30 at the house and the memorial service at 2:00 on the fourteenth at the Daiichi Hall.

MICHAEL:

Sō desu ka. Arigatō gozaimasu. Kato-san wa dō shimasu ka?

そうですか。ありがとうございます。加藤さんはどうしますか。

Thank you for letting me know. What do you plan to do?

KATO:

Sō desu ne. Kokubetsu-shiki dake ni deyō to omotte imasu ga,
そうですね。告別式だけに出ようと思っていますが、
Well, I thought I'd just go to the memorial service.

MICHAEL:

Sō desu ka? Ja, sashi-tsukae ga nakereba, issho ni itte mo ii deshō ka?
そうですか。じゃ、差し支えがなければ、一緒に行ってもいいでしょうか。
I see. If it's not a problem, could I go with you?

KATO:

Sō desu ne. Jā, ichi-ji yonjuppun ni kaijō no robii de aimashō.
そうですね。じゃ、1時40分に会場のロビーで会いましょう。
Not at all. Let's meet in the lobby of the venue at 1:40.

MICHAEL:

Arigatō gozaimasu. O-negai shimasu.
ありがとうございます。お願いします。
*Thank you. I appreciate it. (*lit. *I request.)*

KATO:

Shitsurei shimasu.
失礼します。
Goodbye.

Visiting the Home

If a neighbor, a close friend, or a relative of a close friend dies, you can go at any time to the house to express your condolences. Take a gift of flowers, fruit or cakes; in return, you will probably receive a small gift. Tell the shop assistant that your purchases are for a home altar and they will be wrapped appropriately:

- **Butsudan ni agetain' desu ga,**
  仏壇に上げたいんですが、
  They're for a home altar.

When you reach the house, you will be ushered into a room that the undertakers have transformed with yards of white material. There will be an altar, a photograph of the deceased, candles, and offerings of fruit and cakes. You should bow to the bereaved present your gift, and say the following:

- **Goshūshō-sama de gozaimasu. Go-reizen ni dōzo.**
  ご愁傷様でございます。ご霊前にどうぞ。
  You have my deepest sympathy. This is for the spirit of the departed.

Then proceed to the altar. After bowing your head in prayer, look briefly at the photograph of the deceased. If you wish, you can offer incense. Bow once more, turn to the family, bow, and leave.

13.03 Offering Incense

At the wake and memorial service, people offer incense when paying respects to the deceased. If incense sticks are used, follow this procedure:

1. Bow. Take one or more sticks of incense and light them from the candle.
2. Fan sticks with the left hand to extinguish. Do not blow!
3. Stand the sticks separately in the incense burner.
4. Bow once more.

If powdered incense is used, bow, take a pinch of incense and sprinkle it over the incense burner, and bow once more.

13.04 Expressing Your Condolences

If you watch the ladies in their black kimono, you can see that bows can be far more eloquent than words and generally, a bow is enough, perhaps with the words **kono tabi wa domo** (この度はどうも) petering off into the bow. Still, you may want to express your grief in words:

- **Kono tabi wa goshūshō-sama de gozaimashita.**
  この度はご愁傷様でございました。
  Please accept my deepest sympathy.

- **Kono tabi wa totsuzen na koto de.**
  この度は突然なことで。
  It was so unexpected.

- **Haya-sugite hontō ni zannen deshita.**
  早すぎて本当に残念でした。
  It is most unfortunate. He/she was far too young.

- **Rippa na kata deshita.**
  立派な方でした。
  He was a fine man.

- **Watakushi ni nanika dekiru koto ga arimashitara, go-enryo naku o-mōshitsuke kudasai.**
  私に何かできることがありましたら、ご遠慮なくお申しつけ
  ください。
  If there is anything I can do, please do not hesitate to ask.

13.05   Sending a Telegram

In the past, telegrams of condolence were sent by people who were unable to hurry to the house immediately. Sending telegrams has become even more widespread today. If you can read Japanese, the procedure is very easy and can be done on the internet. Choose a text from the hundreds of examples, something like this:

- **Tsutsushinde aitō no i o hyōshimasu.**
  謹んで哀悼の意を表します。
  Please accept my condolences. (lit. *I respectfully express my condolences.*)

- **Go-seikyo o itami, tsutsushinde o-kuyami mōshi-agemasu.**
  ご逝去を悼み、謹んでお悔やみを申し上げます。
  I grieve over your loss and offer my respectful sympathy.

- **Go-seikyo o itami, go-meifuku o o-inori mōshi-agemasu.**
  ご逝去を悼み、ご冥福をお祈り申し上げます。
  I grieve over your loss and pray that the deceased rests in peace.

13.06 Offering Branches of Sakaki

In a Shinto memorial service, the priest hands each person a branch of the **sakaki** to place on the altar. The procedure for placing the branch on the altar is as follows:

1. Bow once.
2. Turn the branch around clockwise and place it with the stem toward the altar.
3. Bow twice and *silently* clap twice.
4. Bow once more.

13.07 Writing a Letter of Sympathy

Although sending a letter of sympathy is not a Japanese custom, a letter can be a great consolation and if you are living abroad and unable to attend the funeral or send a telegram it may be a good solution.

> Tori-isogi pen o torimashita.
>
> Go-shujin no totsuzen no go-seikyo o ukagai, taihen na odoroki to kanashimi o kanjimashita. Sengetsu o-hanashi shita bakari na no ni, kono yo o satte shimawareta to wa totemo shinjiraremasen.
>
> Go-shujin wa rippa na kata de, mata ii tomo deshita. Shigoto ni wa kibishii kata deshita ga, ningen-sei ga yutaka de, itsumo hito no tame ni isshōkenmei tsukushite imashita. Nihon ni kite kara mada hi ga asai watashi wa go-shujin ni taihen o-sewa ni nari, sono koto wa itsumademo wasuremasen.
>
> Go-seikyo o itami, tsutsushinde o-kuyami mōshi-agemasu.

取り急ぎ、ペンを取りました。

ご主人の突然のご逝去を伺い、たいへんな驚きと悲しみを感じました。先月お話したばかりなのに、この世を去ってしまわれたとはとても信じられません。

ご主人は立派な方で、またいい友でした。仕事には厳しい方でしたが、人間性豊かで、いつも人のために一生懸命つくしていました。日本に来てからまだ日が浅い私はご主人にたいへんお世話になり、そのことはいつまでも忘れません。

ご逝去を悼み、謹んでお悔やみ申し上げます。

I write to you in haste.

I was most shocked and saddened to hear of the sudden death of your husband. It is very hard to believe that he is no longer with us; it was only one month ago that I had talked to him.

Your husband was a fine man and a good friend. Although he was strict at work, he was very caring and always worked hard for other people. I will never forget the unstinting help he gave me during my early days in Japan.

Please accept my most sincere condolences in your bereavement.

13.08   Words and Expressions

fukō ga atta	不幸があった	*someone has died, (lit. something unfortunate has happened.)*
tsuya	通夜	*wake*
sōgi/sōshiki	葬儀・葬式	*funeral*
kokubetsu-shiki	告別式	*funeral service for general mourners*
sōgi ni sanretsu suru	葬儀に参列する	*to attend a funeral*

gasshō	合掌	*Buddhist prayer position for the hands*
go-kiritsu kudasai.	ご起立ください	*please stand.*
go-jūshoku-sama	ご住職様	*Buddhist priest*
o-kyō	お経	*Buddhist sutra*
senkō (o ageru)	線香(を上げる)	*(to offer) an incense stick*
shōkō suru	焼香する	*to offer powdered incense*
ko-~	故	*the late ~*
izoku	遺族	*the bereaved*
sōgi iinchō	葬儀委員長	*chairman of the funeral committee*
moshu	喪主	*chief mourner*
chōji	弔辞	*obituary*
chōden	弔電	*condolence telegram*
o-kuyami	お悔み	*condolence*
saijō	斎場	*funeral parlor*
sōgi-ya	葬儀屋	*undertaker*
hitsugi/o-kan	棺・お棺	*coffin*
reikyūsha	霊柩車	*hearse*
kasō suru	火葬する	*to cremate*
kasōba	火葬場	*crematory*
o-kotsu	お骨	*the ashes*
haka	墓	*grave*
hakaba	墓場	*graveyard (for example in a Buddhist temple)*
reien	霊園	*cemetery*
butsudan	仏壇	*Buddhist home altar*

kaimyō	戒名	*Buddhist name given to a person after death*
isshūki	一周忌	*service on the first anniversary of a death*
sankaiki	三回忌	*service on the second anniversary of a death*
hōyō/hōji	法要・法事	*Buddhist memorial service*
kibiki kyūka	忌引き休暇	*absence from work or school due to mourning*
kōden	香典	*offering of money at a funeral*
kōden dorobō	香典泥棒	*thief, posing as a mourner, who steals funeral offerings*

Ihai-mochi　　いはい持ち

Ihai いはい are the wooden memorial tablets kept in Buddhist home altars. Each tablet bears the posthumous name of a deceased relative. **Ihai-mochi**, which means "keeper of the memorial tablets," is a term used to refer to the eldest son. People may call an eldest son **ihai-mochi** to remind him that one day he will inherit the family altar, the memorial tablets, and the responsibility of carrying on the family name. He may also refer to himself as **ihai-mochi** to show that he is resigned to carrying out his family responsibilities.

Chapter 14 Speeches

Speeches

With the exception of lectures (**kōen**), speeches in Japan are seldom original. In most cases, everybody pretty much knows at the outset what to expect. This is especially true with the short introductory speech referred to as the **go-aisatsu**, which literally means "greeting." Regardless of whether the **go-aisatsu** is a congratulatory message at a reception or an animated pep talk in front of the whole company, people expect the speech to include certain set expressions and to have a certain style and form. If the speech departs from the norm, it might be judged odd and unsettling.

In any given ceremony, each of the many speeches has a specific function—for example, introducing the speakers, stating goals and objectives, thanking people for coming, giving the toast, and closing the ceremony. Sometimes various guests, starting with the VIPs and moving downward, will be called upon to say a few words at large business receptions. In many cases, the less important speeches become the background music against which the guests help themselves to the food served at the elegantly prepared buffet tables.

Let us put serious speeches and lectures aside for a moment and first deal with speeches given at social functions. If you are asked to give a speech, think of it as one piece in the overall structure of the ceremony. Decide whether your speech is a keystone, a supporting block, or a decoration, and adapt the tone and length accordingly. Unless you are the main speaker, great thoughts or verbal pyrotechnics are not expected and would probably be out of place.

The very fact that you are standing up and making a speech in Japanese is quite enough to impress people. In most instances, you do not have to strain yourself to make your presentation unique. Thus, you should try not to spoil your speech by making jokes about Japan, giving one personal opinion after another, or delivering a flood of witty comments or ironic barbs. Too many of these informal comments often will just make a Japanese audience feel uncomfortable.

This is not to say that your speech has to be without humor. Once you have established a properly serious tone and have said all the right things, a little levity can give spark to your speech, so long as it is not at the expense of anyone present. In fact, if you can manage it, a few verbal jokes and puns in Japanese can be very effective. A word of caution though: regardless of whether said in English or in Japanese, Western jokes seldom go over well.

A good speaker in Japan always has lots of thanks to give. Even if he really is the person with all the power, he will say that everyone has been learning and growing together, stress that he has constantly borrowed other people's strengths and wisdom, and protest that he could not do anything without the audience's help and cooperation. Whatever the activity, whether it is managing a neighborhood baseball team or taking over an American bank, a good speaker will insist that it is an effort (**doryoku**) to which everyone can contribute with his or her determination (**ketsui**), devotion (**kenshin**), and tenacity (**shūnen**). Above all, the speaker will stress that the whole activity will be done wholeheartedly (**sshō-kenmei**), with each person giving all that he or she can give (**ganbaru**—or, in more formal settings— **zenshin o agete** or **doryoku shite mairu**).

Furthermore, while the audience may not particularly want to know what you think of your own home country, they will surely be interested to hear what you have noticed about them. Talking of things that are familiar to your audience is the surest way of paying them a compliment. Flattering the person in whose honor you are speaking is, of course, a very good idea. Perhaps you could also think of some local custom, event, or cuisine, and somehow work it in your speech. Sharing your views about a local topic will show your audience that you have taken the time to learn something about them.

Now let us look at serious speeches and lectures. Since people are probably spending time and/or money to hear your opinions, you should not disappoint them by delivering a speech with no substance. The biggest danger is making your speech too complicated. Whether you are speaking in Japanese or through an interpreter, you should expect that twenty percent of what you say will not get through. For one thing, a speech is not an essay, and unless you have an uncommon mastery of Japanese, subtle meanings and nuances will be neither understood nor appreciated by the audience. Therefore, keep your sentences short and punchy and organize your speech so that it concentrates on just a few main points. Your main ideas are often best listed as "Five Points" or "Four Principles," and you should enumerate them, elaborate on them, and then recapitulate them.

One final word of advice: do not be discouraged if your audience adopts a somnolent posture within seconds after you begin your speech. It can happen to any speaker. Sympathize with them, since they may be a drafted audience, and remember that they may not be used to hearing original, thought-provoking speeches. If what you have to say is really important, try to make sure in advance that the speech is available to the audience in written form, or that the press is there and primed with a printed synopsis of the major points. In the majority of cases, however, the fact that you are contributing to the ceremonial procedures of the occasion is the most important thing.

[Note: this chapter introduction appears with the courtesy of Sir Stephen Gomersall.]

Introducing Yourself

Sometimes a gathering may begin with everyone taking turns to introduce themselves, **jiko shōkai** 自己紹介. The basic introduction consists of your name and your affiliation. You can also explain briefly where you come from, how long you've been in Japan, your impressions of the country, your interests, and so on. At informal parties, you can gain instant popularity by showing off your singing ability.

- **Monbu kagakushō ryūgakusei no Rin Bun Ho desu. Dōzo yoroshiku.**

  文部科学省留学生の林文宝です。どうぞよろしく。

  I'm Lin Wenbao and I'm a Japanese government scholarship student. I'm pleased to be here.

Note: 文部科学省 Ministry of Education, Culture, Sports, Science and Technology (MEXT)

- **Ekoshisutemu no Kurisu Jonson desu. Umare wa Nyu Yōku-shū de, rokkagetsu mae ni Nihon ni kimashita. Tokugi wa jūdō desu.**

  エコシステムのクリス・ジョンソンです。生まれはニューヨーク州で、6ヶ月前に日本に来ました。特技は、柔道です。

  I'm Chris Johnson from EcoSystems. I'm from New York State and I came to Japan six months ago. My special skill is judo.

- **Kinguzu Eikaiwa no Buraun desu. Kuni no uta o utaimasu. Iesutadei.**

  キングズ英会話のブラウンです。国の歌を歌います。イエス タデイ。

  I'm Brown from Kings English Conversation. I'll sing you a song from my country: "Yesterday".

14.02 Beginning a Speech

Although the body of a speech is fine in a normal, conversational style, there are conventional phrases that should be used at the beginning and end. The following examples show the kind of language to use when standing up in front of an audience. Notice that they all follow the same pattern: introduce yourself, state your relationship to the guest or the event, and then state the purpose of your speech.

- **Mina-sama, konban wa. Kankoku kara mairimashita Kimu de gozaimasu. Watashi to Yoshiko-san wa kōkō no toki kara no tsukiai desu. Kyō, o-iwai no kotoba o nobesasete itadakimasu.**

  皆様、こんばんは。韓国から参りました金でございます。私 と良子さんは高校の時からの付き合いです。今日、お祝い の言葉を述べさせていただきます。

  Good evening, everyone. My name is Kim and I've come from South Korea. Yoshiko and I have known each other since high school. Today I'd like to say a few words of congratulation.

- **Go-shōkai arigatō gozaimashita. Emiri Tērā to mōshimasu. Jimukyoku o daihyō itashimashite, mina-sama ni o-rei no go-aisatsu o mōshiagemasu.**

  ご紹介ありがとうございました。エミリ・テーラーと申しま す。事務局を代表いたしまして、皆様にお礼のご挨拶を申 し上げます。

Thank you for the introduction. My name is Emily Taylor. On behalf of the organizers, I would like to say a few words of thanks.

- **Tadaima go-shōkai azukarimashita Makkusu Buraun desu. Igirisu shusshin desu. Gonen mae kara Sendai-shi de eigo o oshiete imasu. Maemae kara, Okada-sensei ga, "Anata no keiken wa omoshiroi hanashi ni naru ni chigainai" to itte oraremashita ga, minasama no sankō ni nareba, yōyaku hikiukemashita. Kyō wa yoroshiku o-negai itashimasu.**
ただいまご紹介あずかりましたマックス・ブラウンです。イギリス出身です。5年前から仙台市で英語を教えています。前々から、岡田先生が、「あなたの経験は面白い話になるに違いない」と言っておられましたが、皆様の参考になればと、ようやく引き受けました。今日はよろしくお願いいたします。
Thank you for the introduction. I'm Max Brown and I'm from the UK. I've been teaching English in Sendai for the past five years. For quite a while, Okada-sensei has been telling me that my experiences would make an interesting talk. Thinking that it might be useful to you, I finally agreed. I look forward to spending time with you today.

This is an introduction to a speech in English. Pause over the word **yaya** (slightly) for effect.

- **Go-shōkai arigatō gozaimashita. Ekoshisutemu no Jonson de gozaimasu. Kyō mina-sama ni kono yō ni o-hanashi dekiru koto wa taihen kōei de gozaimasu. Kono jū-nenkan, gokai mo rainichi shi, Nihongo mo naganen benkyō itashimashita. Shikashi, mada eigo no hō ga yaya tokui na no de, kyō no kōen wa eigo de sasete itadakimasu. Dewa, tsūyaku o-negai itashimasu.**
ご紹介ありがとうございました。エコシステムのジョンソンでございます。今日、皆様にこのようにお話できることはたいへん光栄でございます。この10年間、5回も来日し、日本語も長年勉強いたしました。しかし、まだ英語の方がやや

得意なので、今日の講演は英語でさせていただきます。で
は、通訳お願いいたします。

Thank you for the introduction. My name is Johnson, and I'm from EcoSystems. It is a great honor to be able to speak with you today. Although this is already my fifth visit to Japan during the last ten years, and in spite of the fact that I have spent considerable time studying Japanese, I still speak English slightly better than Japanese. For that reason I would like to give today's lecture in English. So, if the interpreter is ready. . .

This is how to address the chair at formal meetings:

- **Gichō, go-resseki no mina-samagata.**
  議長、ご列席の皆様方
  Chairperson, ladies and gentlemen.

When acknowledging people by name, use their surnames and titles as much as possible:

- **Matsudaira Chiji, Yamazaki Kaichō, minamina-sama.**
  松平知事、山崎会長、皆々様
  Governor Matsudaira, Chairman Yamazaki, ladies and gentlemen.

14.03 Ending a Speech

To end a short speech, you can simply thank the audience, bow, and return to your seat. For longer speeches, it's customary to express appreciation for the audience's attention and to apologize that your speech was not very good.

- **Kantan de gozaimasu ga, watakushi kara no go-aisatsu to sasete itadakimasu.**
  簡単でございますが、私からのご挨拶とさせていただきます。
  These are just a few words, but I offer them as my speech.

- **Chōjikan go-seichō arigatō gozaimashita.**
  長時間、ご静聴ありがとうございました。
  Thank you for your attention for such a long time.

- **Kyō no watashi no hanashi ga sukoshi demo go-sankō ni nareba, ureshiku omoimasu. Arigatō gozaimashita.**
  今日の私の話が少しでもご参考になれば、うれしく思います。ありがとうございました。
  I hope that my talk today has been helpful to you. Thank you very much.

14.04 Giving a Thank-you Speech

At a farewell party, the leader of a group expresses thanks to the organizers of a tour.

Mina-sama, konban wa. Gurūpu riidā to shite, hito-koto o-rei no go-aisatsu o mōshiagemasu.

Wazuka yokka-kan de Tōkyō, Ōsaka, Nara o mawari, Nihon no nagai bunka to saishin no gijutsu ni fureru koto ga dekimashita.

Isogashii nittei de wa arimashita ga, minna no o-kage de, tsuā ga daiseikō. Suponsā no "Yoi Kankyō kabushikikaisha" sama ni kansha o mōshi-agemasu. Kobayashi-sama, arigatō gozaimashita.

Mina-sama no atatakai o-motenashi ni kokoro kara o-rei o mōshiagemasu. Watakushidomo wa ashita kaerimasu. Okage-sama de Nihon no koto ga sukoshi wakatta yō na ki ga shimasu. Mata kitai to omoimasu. Mina-sama o-genki de o-sugoshi kudasai.

Hontō ni arigatō gozaimashita.

皆様、こんばんは。グループ・リーダーとして、ひとことお礼のご挨拶を申し上げます。

わずか四日間で東京、大阪、奈良を回り、日本の長い文化と最新の技術にふれることができました。忙しい日程ではありましたが、皆のおかげで、ツアーが大成功。スポンサーの「よい環境株式会社」様に感謝を申し上げます。小林様、ありがとうございました。

皆様の暖かいおもてなしに心からお礼を申し上げます。私どもは明日帰ります。お蔭さまで日本のことが少し分かったような気がします。また、来たいと思います。皆様、お元気でお過ごしください。

本当にありがとうございました。

Good evening, ladies and gentlemen. As the group leader I would like to say a few words of thanks.

Although we had only four days to visit Tokyo, Osaka, and Nara, this still gave us the chance to see both Japan's ancient culture and its most modern technology. Even though it was a very busy schedule, thanks to you all, the tour was a great success. I would like to thank the sponsor, Yoi Kankyo (Good Environment) plc. Thank you, Mr Kobayashi.

Our sincere thanks also go to all of you for your warm hospitality. We must leave tomorrow, but thanks to you, we feel that we have gotten to understand Japan a little better. We would like to come again. Take care of yourselves. Thank you very much indeed.

Giving a Welcome Speech

14.05

In this speech, Michael welcomes prospective clients to a seminar and luncheon. He uses humble verbs to introduce the main speaker because both of them are members of the same organization. This does not preclude him, however, from impressing the guests with his boss's credentials.

Mina-sama, ohayō gozaimasu. Honjitsu wa o-isogashii tokoro o "Chikyu ondanka" ni kansuru kono seminā ni go-shusseki itadaki, arigatō gozaimasu.

Watashi wa Ekoshisutemu no Nihon daihyō no Tērā Maikeru desu. Heisha wa Gurōbaru Shisutemu no kankyō bumon de ari, torihiki no chūshin wa Nyū Yōku, Tōkyō, Pekin to natte orimasu. Kono yon-nenkan, Tōkyō no daihyōbu wa mina-sama no niizu ni kotaeru beku doryoku shite mairimashita. Kongotomo, sue-nagai minori aru torihiki o kitai shite orimasu.

Kyō no mēn supiikā wa heisha no jōmu no Debiddo Ebanzu de gozaimasu. Jōmu wa Amerika de wa yūmei na kenkyūka de, Hābādo daigaku o sotsugyō-go, nijūgo nenkan kankyō gyōmu ni tsuite kimashita. Jōmu kara shingijutsu no shōkai to, toku ni Nihon no tōshika ni totte sono igi ni tsuite, go-setsumei mō-shiagemasu.

Kono seminā ga owarimashitara, tonari ni sasayaka na chūshoku no yōi o itashite orimasu no de, go-kandan kudasaimase. Nao, o-kaeri no sai ni, Nihongo no shiryō o o-kubari itashimasu. Kyō wa go-shusseki kudasaimashite, arigatō gozaimashita.

皆様、おはようございます。本日はお忙しいところを「地球温暖化」に関するこのセミナーにご出席いただき、ありがとうございます。

私はエコシステムの日本代表のマイケル・テーラーです。弊社はグローバル・システムの環境部門であり、取引の中心はニ

ューヨーク・東京・北京となっております。この４年間、東京の代表部は皆様のニースに答えるべく努力してまいりました。今後とも、末永い実りある取引を期待しております。

今日のメーンスピーカーは弊社の常務のデビッド・エバンズでございます。常務はアメリカでは有名な研究家で、ハーバード大学を卒業後、25年間環境業務に就いてきました。常務から新技術の紹介と、特に日本の投資家にとってその意義について、ご説明申し上げます。

このセミナーが終わりましたら、隣にささやかな昼食の用意をしておりますので、ご歓談くださいませ。なお、お帰りの際に、日本語の資料をお配りいたします。今日はご出席くださいまして、ありがとうございました。

Good morning ladies and gentlemen. Thank you very much for sparing the time to join us today at this seminar on "Climate Change".

My name is Michael Taylor, and I am Japan representative of Eco-Systems. The company is the environment arm of Global Systems and has its centers of business in New York, Tokyo and Beijing. In Tokyo, our representative office has worked hard to fulfil your needs during the last four years and we look forward to a long and fruitful business relationship with you in the future.

Our main speaker today is my colleague, Mr. David Evans, managing director. Mr. Evans, a well-known researcher in the US, is a graduate of Harvard University, and has been involved in the environment business for twenty-five years. He is here today to tell us about new technology and what this means for the Japanese investor.

After the seminar, we hope that you will join us for a light lunch in the next room. Also, as you leave we will be giving you a selection of written materials in Japanese.

Thank you again for being with us today.

Proposing a Toast

The toast signals an end to the speeches and a start to the food and drink. While you can add personal comments to the examples below, toasts should be kept brief. First, here's a toast given by a boss at an office year-end party:

- **Ichinenkan no go-doryoku ni kansha shi, rainen no masu-masu no hatten o inotte, kanpai!**
  1年間のご努力に感謝し、来年のますますの発展を祈って、乾杯！
  Thank you for your efforts throughout the year. Here's to even greater success next year. Cheers!

These next two are for more formal occasions:

- **Yoi Kankyō kabushiki kaisha no masu-masu no go-hatten to nit'chū ryōkoku no kagiri-naki yūjō ni. Kanpai!**
  「よい環境株式会社」のますますのご発展と日中両国の限りなき友情に。乾杯！
  To the further growth of Good Environment plc and to eternal friendship between Japan and China. Cheers!

- Dewa, kanpai no ondo o torasete itadakimasu. Go-sankai no mina-sama no go-kenshō to kore-kara no go-katsuyaku o inori, kanpai shitai to omoimasu. Mina-sama, go-shōwa o-negai itashimasu. Kanpai!

では、乾杯の音頭をとらせていただきます。ご参会の皆様のご健勝とこれからのご活躍を祈り、乾杯したいと思います。皆様、ご唱和お願いいたします。乾杯！

I would like to propose a toast. Please raise your glasses to the good health and continued prosperity of all present. All together, please. Cheers!

14.07 Words and Expressions

go-aisatsu	ご挨拶	*short introductory speech*
jiko shōkai	自己紹介	*self-introduction*
supiichi	スピーチ	*speech (usually informal)*
kōen	講演	*talk, lecture*
zadankai	座談会	*discussion meeting, round table conference*
kanpai suru	乾杯する	*to make a toast*
endai	演題	*title of a speech*
endan	演壇	*rostrum*
kinchō suru	緊張する	*to get nervous*
agaru	あがる	*to get stage fright*

Chapter 15 E-mail and Letters

E-mail and Letters

The computer and e-mail are a godsend for non-native speakers of Japanese, first by liberating us from writing **kanji** which, since most of us did not spend our formative years learning to write them, can be painstaking and slow and, secondly, by sparing us the embarrassment of poor handwriting that belies our otherwise good knowledge of the language. In addition to straightforward word-processing features, which give us access to a wide vocabulary and let us write complex characters in an instant, we can now print out postcards and letters of a standard we could only have dreamed of in the days when they had to be handwritten.

Although communication is much easier and messaging has become increasingly brief and instant, e-mails have an important role to play in business communication and also provide a lasting record. It is obviously important whenever you write an e-mail that you choose your words carefully and re-read your message before hitting the send button. Here I hope to show you how Japanese e-mails are constructed and give you words and phrases you can adapt for your own use.

Japanese business e-mails, especially those to customers and people outside the company, seem to follow a certain form that is rather like the **go-aisatsu** we saw in the chapter on speeches, So, e-mails often start with a **jiko shōkai** (self introduction) followed by set phrases to mark the beginning of the message, then, after the main body of the message, set phrases to close. Although the structure is slightly different from that of a letter, many of the phrases used come from traditional letter writing. Especially in business communication the language can be very formal indeed but I have tried to give examples that are polite without sounding stuffy.

The main time of the year when people put pen to paper is in December, during the buildup to the holiday season. I have given examples of phrases you could add to your holiday cards or e-messages and, for those of you residing in Japan, some ideas for New Year cards. These are postcards and they are delivered all together on New Year's Day (just make sure they are marked 年賀 (**nenga** New Year's greeting) on the address side.

Until recently, people would make their own woodblock prints, or write each card by hand in calligraphy, or order printed cards. Now there is a wide variety available, most featuring the Chinese zodiac animal for the coming year. Cards bought at the post office have numbers printed on them; you might win a prize in the lottery. Or you can download or purchase software and have fun creating your own cards incorporating photos or mixing and matching different images and text. When it comes to sending the cards most people write in a sentence or two to make the card more personal.

Having said all this, a letter or postcard handwritten in the traditional way is very personal and would impress your Japanese acquaintances greatly. If you want to give it a try, here are some suggestions to improve your writing. Buy paper or cards with lines on, broader lines rather than narrow. Then, draw a faint line in pencil down the center of each column (erase it after you've finished writing). Try to center each kanji on this line. The vertical strokes should be straight down, top to bottom, but when writing the horizontal strokes try making the lines slant slightly upwards towards the right. Good luck!

15.01 Internal E-mail Messages
mēru メール

E-mails to colleagues can be short and to the point. They are often prefaced with the greeting お疲れ様 です (**o-tsukare-sama desu** Thank you for your help). Here, Michael sends some data to his colleague for a report they are writing.

送信者　　：〈m.taylor@ecosystems.co.jp〉
宛先　　　：〈y.sato@ecosystems.co.jp〉
送信日時　：〈2011年8月26日　09.21〉
添付　　　：市場データ.xls
件名　　　：市場調査の件

お疲れ様です。
データを添付します。
質問などありましたら、今日中にご返信をお願いします。
よろしくお願いします。
テーラー

Sōshinsha　：<m.taylor@ecosystems.co.jp>
Atesaki　：<y.sato@ ecosystems.co.jp>
Sōshin nichiji：<nisen jūichi nen hachigatsu nijūroku nichi 09.21>
Tenpu　：Shijō dēta.xls
Kenmei　：Shijō chōsa no ken

O-tsukare-sama desu.
Dēta o tenpu shimasu.
Shitsumon nado arimashitara, kyō-jū ni go-henshin o o-negai shimasu.
Yoroshiku o-negai shimasu.
Tērā

Sender : *<m.taylor@ecosystems.co.jp>*
Recipient : *<y.sato@ecosystems.co.jp>*
Date sent : *<26 August 2011   09.21>*
Attachment : *Market Data.xls*
Subject : *Re: Market Survey*

Thank you for your help.
I'm attaching the data.
If you have any questions, please reply to me today.
I appreciate your cooperation.
Taylor

A couple of days later Yumi finishes the report and sends it to Michael, asking for his confirmation and approval.

送信者　　：〈y.sato@ecosystems.co.jp〉
宛先　　　：〈m.taylor@ecosystems.co.jp〉
送信日時：〈2011年8月28日　17.11〉
添付　　　：市場調査.doc
件名　　　：ご連絡

お疲れ様です。
市場調査ができましたので、送付します。
内容を確認の上、ご承認願います。
佐藤

Sōshinsha : <y.sato@ecosystems.co.jp>
Atesaki : <m.taylor@ecosystems.co.jp>
Sōshin nichiji: <nisen jūichi nen hachigatsu nijūhachi nichi 17.11>
Tenpu : Shijō chōsa.doc
Kenmei : Go-renraku

O-tsukaresama desu.
Shijō chōsa ga dekimashita no de, sōfu shimasu.
Naiyō o kakunin no ue, go-shōnin negaimasu.
Satō

Sender : <m.taylor@ecosystems.co.jp>
Recipient : <y.sato@ ecosystems.co.jp>
Date sent : <28 August 2011   17.11>
Attachment : Market Survey.doc
Subject : For your information

Thank you for your help.
I have finished the market survey and am sending it.
Please check the contents and give your approval.
Sato

External E-mail Communication

Michael sends an e-mail to Mr Takahashi thanking him for his time and following up on the results of the meeting. Note the **jiko shōkai** (self introduction) and words of thanks at the beginning, and the conventional phrases used to close.

送信者　：〈m.taylor@ecosystems.co.jp〉
宛先　　：〈k.takahashi@ dmc.co.jp〉
送信日時：〈2012年2月10日　17.15〉
件名　　：　御礼

高橋幸一様
エコシステムのテーラーです。
本日は　お忙しい中、わざわざお時間をいただき、
誠にありがとうございました。

今回、ご指摘いただきました点は、早速、開発部と相談し、
ご要望に添うことができますよう検討中でございます。
今月中には、新たな提案をしたいと思います。

また、何かございましたら、いつでもご連絡ください。
今後とも、よろしくお願いいたします。

Sōshinsha   : <m.taylor@ecosystems.co.jp>
Atesaki   : <k.takahashi@ dmc.co.jp>
Sōshin nichiji : <nisen jūni nen nigatsu tōka 17.15>
Kenmei   : On-rei

Takahashi Kōichi-sama
Ekoshisutemu no Tērā desu.
Honjitsu wa o-isogashii naka, wazawaza o-jikan o itadaki
makoto ni arigatō gozaimashita.

Konkai, go-shiteki itadakimashita ten wa, sassoku kaihatsubu
to sōdan shi, go-yōbō ni sōu koto ga dekimasu yō kentōchū de
gozaimasu. Kongetsu-chū ni wa, arata na teian o shitai to
omoimasu.

Mata, nanika gozaimashitara, itsudemo go-renraku kudasai.
Kongotomo, yoroshiku o-negai itashimasu.

Sender   : <m.taylor@ecosystems.co.jp>
Recipient : <k.takahashi@ dmc.co.jp>
Date sent : <10 February 2012   17.15>
Subject   : Thank you

Mr Koichi Takahashi
This is Taylor of EcoSystems.
*Thank you very much for making time to see us today when you are
so busy.*

*Regarding the points that you raised, I have already consulted our
development department and we are looking into the matter with a
view to meeting your requirements. I hope to have a new proposal
for you this month.*

If there is anything else, please contact me at any time.
We look forward to a continued association.

In this e-mail, Michael tries to get a reply to an e-mail he sent some time ago.

送信者　　：〈m.taylor@ecosystems.co.jp〉
宛先　　　：〈m.kobayashi@yoikankyo.co.jp〉
送信日時：〈2012年3月5日　09.10〉
件名　　　：新規事業について

よい環境株式会社　営業部
小林治様

エコシステムのテーラーです。
お世話になっております。

先月のメールの件について、ご連絡いたします。是非10月より
スタートできればと進めておりますが、

予算、スケジュールについて、なるべく早く、
打ち合わせをしたいと思います。

お忙しいかと思いますが、ご検討、よろしくお願いいたします。
お返事お待ちしております。

Sōshinsha　　　: <m.taylor@ecosystems.co.jp>
Atesaki　　　　: <m.kobayashi@yoikankyo.co.jp>
Sōshin nichiji : <nisen jūni nen sangatsu itsuka 09.10>
Kenmei　　　　: Shinki jigyō ni tsuite

Yoi kankyō kabushikigaisha Eigyōbu
Kobayashi Osamu-sama

Ecoshisutemu no Tērā desu.
O-sewa ni natte orimasu.

Sengetsu no mēru no ken ni tsuite, go-renraku itashimasu. Zehi jūgatsu yori sutāto dekireba to susumete orimasu ga, yosan, sukejūru ni tsuite narubeku hayaku, uchiawase shitai to omoi-masu.

O-isogashii ka to omoimasu ga, go-kentō, yoroshiku o-negai itashimasu.
O-henji o-machi shite orimasu.

Sender   : <m.taylor@ecosystems.co.jp>
Recipient : <m.kobayashi@yoikankyo.co.jp>
Date sent : <5 March 2012   09.10>
Subject   : Re: New Project

Good Environment Co. Ltd., Sales Department
Mr Osamu Kobayashi

This is Taylor of EcoSystems.
We are much obliged to you.

I am contacting you regarding the matter mentioned in my message last month. We really would like to make a start in October if possible and we would like a meeting as soon as possible [to discuss] the budget and the schedule.

I realize you are very busy, but I would appreciate your looking into this.
I look forward to hearing from you.

15.03   More E-mail Language

Now that you have seen some typical e-mails in Japanese and understood how they are constructed, here are some variations you can use on different occasions.

Opening phrases

As we've seen in the examples above, it is usual to state the name of the person you are sending the message to, with or without the name of the company and his or her position. If you're sending the message to several people start with one of these:

- 皆様 ／ 会員の皆様 ／ 委員会の皆様
  Minasama / Kai-in no minasama / Iinkai no minasama
  To everyone / To all members / To all committee members

Then introduce yourself:

- 金英姫です。ソールからメールを送っています。
  Kimu Yun Hee desu. Sōru kara mēru o okutte imasu.
  It's Kim Young Hee. I'm sending this message from Seoul.

Then add one of these follow-up phrases, or any of the general phrases given in the opening chapter of this book:

- いつもお世話になっております。
  Itsumo o-sewa ni natte orimasu
  We are much obliged to you.

- メールありがとうございました。
  Mēru arigatō gozaimashita
  Thank you for your message.

- 初めてメールさせていただきます。
  Hajimete mēru sasete itadakimasu
  This is the first time I am contacting you.

Then state the reason for your message, and any other points you want to make.

- 日本滞在の日程について、ご連絡します。
  Nihon taizai no nittei ni tsuite, go-renraku shimasu.
  I'm contacting you about the schedule for my stay in Japan.

- 先日の会議について、ご報告します。
  Senjitsu no kaigi ni tsuite, go-hōkoku shimasu.
  This is to report on the meeting the other day.

- 進捗状況について、お知らせします。
  Shinchoku jōkyō ni tsuite, o-shirase shimasu.
  This is to let you know how things are progressing.

- ご覧になりましたら、ご一報ください。
  Go-ran ni narimashitara, go-ippō kudasai.
  When you've had a look at this, please get in touch.

- お手数ですが、折り返しご返信をお願いします。
  O-tesū desu ga, orikaeshi go-henshin o o-negai shimasu.
  Sorry to trouble you, but please reply by return.

- 返信不要です。
  Henshin fuyō desu.
  No need to reply

Closing phrases

The message is finished off with the same phrases as those used in traditional letter writing, thanking the recipient, reiterating the nature of the relationship and perhaps briefly stating once more the reason for the message.

- よろしくお願いします。
  Yoroshiku o-negai shimasu.
  Please give this your kind consideration.

- ご検討 / ご協力 / よろしくお願いします。
  Go-kentō / go-kyōryoku yoroshiku o-negai shimasu.
  I ask for your consideration / cooperation.

- まずはメールにてお礼まで / お願いまで / お知らせまで
  Mazu wa mēru nite o-rei made / o-negai made / o-shirase made.
  This message is to express thanks/to ask a favor/for your information.

15.04 A Notice by E-mail   tsūchi   通知

This e-mail, in layout very much like a traditional postcard, shows how to construct an invitation or announcement in Japanese. After the **jiko shōkai** and the reason for the communication, the details of the event are given in list format under the heading 記 (**ki**, to write, record).

盆栽協会の皆様
事務局の金英姫です。
お世話になっております。

慣例の忘年会を下記の通り開催いたします。
多数参加されますようご案内申し上げます。

　　　　　　　　記
日時：12月20日（土）午後6時より
場所：国際ホテル5階　中華レストラン
会費：5000円（夕食、飲み放題）

お手数ですが、出欠席は12月18日までにご連絡ください。
以上、メールにてご案内いたします。

Bonsai kyōkai no minasama
Jimukyoku no Kimu Yun Hee desu.
O-sewa ni natte orimasu.

Kanrei no bōnenkai o kaki no tōri kaisai itashimasu.
Tasū sanka saremasu yō go-annai mōshiagemasu.

Ki

Nichiji : jūnigatsu hatsuka (do), gogo rokuji yori
Basho : Kokusai Hoteru, gokai, Chūka resutoran
Kaihi : gosen-en (yūshoku, nomi-hōdai)
O-tesū desu ga, shukkesseki wa jūnigatsu jūhachi-nichi
made ni go-renraku kudasai.
Ijō , mēru nite go-annai itashimasu.

Members of the Bonsai Society
This is Kim Young Hee, the organizer.
I thank you for your cooperation.

The customary year-end party will be held as shown below.
We hope many people will attend.

Notice

Date and time : December 20th (Sat.), from 6:00 p.m.
Place   : International Hotel, 5th Floor, Chinese restaurant
Cost   : ¥5,000 (dinner and unlimited drinks)

Please reply by December 18th.
This e-mail is to give you the details above.

15.05   Christmas Cards

Here are some phrases you could include in a card or e-message to friends in Japan. If you want to wish your friends a happy new year, use the phrase (良いお年を) **Yoi o-toshi o**. The phrase (明けましておめでとうございます) **Akemashite omedetō gozaimasu** is used only if the card reaches the recipient on or after January 1.

- ハッピーホリデー！
  ご無沙汰しております。当方、家族そろって元気です。機会があれば、いらしてください。ＪＦＫ空港から1時間です。良いお年を。

  Happi horidē!
  Go-busata shite orimasu. Tōhō kazoku sorotte genki desu. Kikai ga areba, irashite kudasai. JFK kūkō kara ichijikan desu. Yoi o-toshi o.

  Happy Holidays!
  Sorry not to have been in touch. The family here are all well. Come and see us if you have the chance. We're an hour from JFK airport. Happy New Year.

- 楽しいクリスマスとすばらしい新年を迎えられますように。

  Tanoshii Kurisumasu to subarashii shinnen o mukaeraremasu yō ni.

  With all good wishes for a merry Christmas and a wonderful new year.

15.06   Family Newsletter

Here's an example of family news you could include with your holiday greetings:

家族の近況
マイケル　　　　　：今年こそ体力づくり
エミリ　　　　　　：早いもので日本の生活も4年目を迎えます。NPO法人の活動をしています。
エレナ(9歳)　　　：すっかり東京弁になりました
ジョン(7歳)　　　：野球に夢中です。
カタリン(1歳6ヶ月)：水泳が得意です。

Kazoku no kinkyō:

Maikeru	: **Kotoshi koso tairyoku-zukuri.**
Emiri	: **Hayai mono de Nihon no seikatsu mo yonen-me o mukaemasu. NPO hōjin no katsudō o shi-te imasu.**
Erena (kyūsai)	: **Sukkari Tokyo-ben ni narimashita**
Jon (nana-sai)	: **Yakyū ni muchū desu.**
Katarin (issai rokkagetsu)	: **Suiei ga tokui desu.**

The family news

Michael	: *Going to get in shape this year.*
Catherine	: *Time goes so quickly. This will be our fourth year in Japan. I am working with a non-profit organisation.*
Eleanor (9)	: *She's got a Tokyo accent..*
John (7)	: *He's mad about baseball.*
Catherine (1 year 6 months)	: *She's a good swimmer.*

15.07 New Year Cards
nengajo 年賀状

New Year cards, when they first appeared in 1873, were written on New Year's Day, and it is still the custom to date the cards 元旦 **gantan**, the first of January. This can be slightly confusing since when you write the cards in early December you have to refer to the current year as the old year 昨年 **sakunen**, and the new year as this year 今年 **kotoshi**.

Families who have had a death during the year send out cards by the end of November explaining that they will not be sending New Year cards. It is standard practice to forgo sending cards to these families.

Here are two examples of the basic wording on a typical New Year card but the possibilities are infinite.

New Year card 1

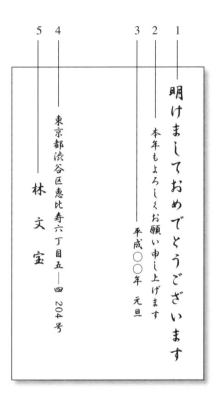

1. Akemashite omedetō gozaimasu
2. Honnen mo yoroshiku o-negai mōshiagemasu.
3. Heisei ○○nen gantan
4. Tokyo-to Shibuya-ku Ebisu 6-chome 5 – 4, 204
5. Rin Bun Ho

1. *Happy New Year.*
2. *Looking forward to continuing our acquaintance this year.*
3. *New Year's Day, the ○○th year of Heisei*
4. *204, 6 – 5 – 4 Ebisu, Shibuya-ku, Tokyo*
5. *Lin Wenbao*

New Year Card 2

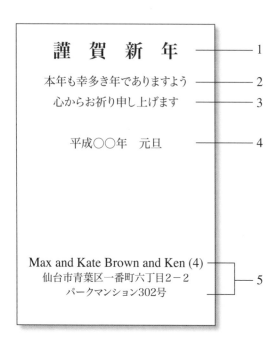

謹　賀　新　年　————— 1

本年も幸多き年でありますよう　————— 2

心からお祈り申し上げます　————— 3

平成〇〇年　元旦　————— 4

Max and Kate Brown and Ken (4)
仙台市青葉区一番町六丁目2－2
パークマンション302号　————— 5

1. Kinga Shinnen
2. Honnen mo shiawase ōki toshi de arimasu yō
3. kokoro kara o-inori mōshiagemasu.
4. Heisei 〇〇nen gantan
5. Sendai-shi Aoba-ku Ichiban-chō, rokuchōme 2 – 2
   Pāku Manshon 302-gō

1. Happy New Year
2–3. With sincere wishes for a very happy new year
4. New Year's Day, the 〇〇th year of Heisei
5. 302 Park Mansion, 6 – 2 – 2 Ichiban-cho, Aoba-ku, Sendai

Here's a selection of phrases you could handwrite on the cards if you want to—just to make them a bit more personal:

- お元気ですか。お幸せな年でありますように。
  O-genki desu ka? O-shiawase na toshi de arimasu yō ni.
  How are you? Hope it will be a happy year for you.

- 今年はぜひお会いしたいですね。
  Kotoshi wa zehi o-ai shitai desu ne.
  I really hope we can get together this year.

- 遊びにいらしてください。
  Asobi ni irashite kudasai.
  Please come and see us

- ご健勝をお祈りいたします。
  Go-kenshō o o-inori itashimasu.
  Wishing you the best of health.

- 昨年はお世話になりました。今年もよろしくお願いいたします。
  Sakunen wa o-sewa ni narimashita. Kotoshi mo yoroshiku o-negai itashimasu.
  We were much indebted to you last year. We look forward to continuing our relationship this year.

- 今年もますますのご活躍を祈っております。
  Kotoshi mo masu-masu no go-katsuyaku o inotte orimasu.
  Wishing you an even better (business) year this year.

What should you do if you receive a card from someone you didn't send one to? Simply send the person a card, including at the end of your usual holiday message this note:

- 早々とお年賀をいただき、ありがとうございました。
  Haya-baya to o-nenga o itadaki, arigatō gozaimashita.
  Thank you for your [early] New Year card.

Formal Postcards
hagaki 葉書

Notes of thanks are traditionally written on postcards and if you have Japanese software you can choose an attractive font and produce perfectly acceptable cards. The standard card measures 148 mm by 100 mm and you should aim for seven or eight lines with between sixteen to nineteen characters per line. In this example which is traditional and quite formal, a woman writes to express thanks for a gift. The closing word, kashiko, which roughly translates as "sincerely", is used only by women; men should use 早々 **sōsō** or 敬具 **keigu**.

Formal postcard

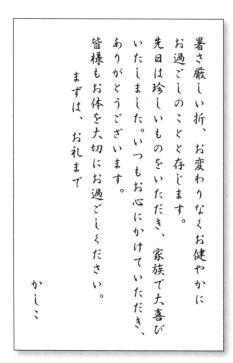

暑さ厳しい折、お変わりなくお健やかに
お過ごしのことと存じます。
先日は珍しいものをいただき、家族で大喜び
いたしました。いつもお心にかけていただき、
ありがとうございます。
皆様もお体を大切にお過ごしください。
まずは、お礼まで

かしこ

Atsusa kibishii ori, o-kawari naku o-sukoyaka ni o-sugoshi no koto to zonjimasu. Senjitsu wa mezurashii mono o itadaki, kazoku de ōyorokobi itashimashita. Itsumo o-kokoro ni kakete itadaki, arigatō gozaimasu. Mina-sama mo o-karada o taisetsu ni o-sugoshi kudasai.
Mazu wa o-rei made.
Kashiko

I am glad to hear that you are well and in good health despite the extreme heat.
The whole family was overjoyed to receive your wonderful gift the other day. We are happy to know that you are always thinking of us.
Please take care of yourselves.
With our thanks.
Sincerely,

Addressing Postcards

With postcards, the addresses of both the recipient and the sender usually go on the same side of the card. Fortunately, these too are a cinch with the right software.

Address side of formal postcard

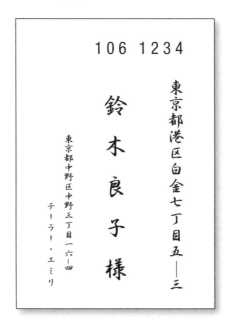

Tokyo-to Minato-ku Shirogane nana-chōme go no san
Suzuki Yoshiko-sama
Tokyo-to Nakano-ku Nakano san- chōme jūroku no yon
Tērā Emiri
Mrs Yoshiko Suzuki
7 – 5 – 3 Shirogane, Minato-ku, Tokyo
Emily Taylor
3 – 16 – 4 Nakano, Nakano-ku, Tokyo

Formal Letters tegami 手紙

Japanese letters differ from English letters in many ways. The name of the recipient and the date come at the end of a letter instead of at the beginning, and letters usually open with cryptic seasonal greetings that poetically allude to the burgeoning green of spring or the fresh snowfall on distant mountaintops. Personal letters which were often works of art both in the feelings expressed and in the calligraphy and overall layout on the paper are now, sadly, a rarity. The language of the traditional letter lives on in formal business correspondence although these are arid by comparison: the writing is horizontal left to right, the seasonal greetings selected by the computer according to the date, and the letters printed out on A4 paper. Non-native speakers will probably not have to write such letters, so I restrict my comments to an explanation of the form and give examples of letters you might write to friends and acquaintances.

Salutations

Salutations are not essential in Japanese letters. But in more formal letters especially, different salutations, all of which correspond to the English "Dear – " are used depending on the type of letter. These are the two most common:

Haikei 拝啓 *Respectfully*

Used on formal letters and postcards. Women use this only when they write business letters. The corresponding closing word is 敬具 **Keigu** Respectfully yours

Zenryaku 前略 *Preliminaries omitted*

Used on short letters and postcards. You don't need to follow it with a seasonal greeting. The corresponding closing word is 早々 (**sōsō** In haste), although women sometimes use かしこ (**kashiko** with respect) or さようなら (**Sayōnara** goodbye).

Opening Phrases

These phrases may be used after or instead of the salutation:

- はじめてお手紙を差し上げます。
  Hajimete o-tegami o sashi-agemasu.
  This is the first time that I am writing to you.

- たいへんご無沙汰しておりますが、お変わりありませんか。
  Taihen go-busata shite orimasu ga, o-kawari arimasen ka?
  I'm sorry not to have written. I hope all is well.

Next comes a seasonal greeting, often followed by an inquiry into the other person's health, for example:

- だんだん春めいてきましたが、お変わりなくお過ごしでしょうか。
  Dan-dan haru-meite kimashita ga, o-kawari naku o-sugoshi desho ka?
  It's getting more like spring; I hope you are well.

- ワシントンは桜が満開です。
  Washinton wa sakura ga mankai desu.
  The cherry blossoms are in full bloom in Washington.

- 初夏のような暖かさが続いております。
  Shoka no yō na atatakasa ga tsuzuite orimasu.
  The weather has been warm, as if it were early summer.

- 書中お見舞い申し上げます。
  Shochū o-mimai mōshi-agemasu.
  Midsummer greetings. (July and August)

- 残暑お見舞い申し上げます。
  Zansho o-mimai mōshi-agemasu.
  Late summer greetings. (late August through early September)

- 東京は蒸し暑い日が続いていますが、いかがお過ごしでしょうか。
  Tōkyō wa mushi-atsui hi ga tsuzuite imasu ga, ikaga o-su-goshi desho ka?
  It has been so hot and humid in Tokyo recently, how are you?

- ニューイングランドも見事な紅葉になりました。
  Nyū Ingurando mo migoto na kōyō ni narimashita.
  The colors of the leaves in New England have become very beautiful.

- すでに師走となりました。
  Sude ni shiwasu to narimashita.
  It's already the end of the year.

This greeting could be used at any time of the year:

- 不順なお天気 / 良い天気 が続いています。
  Fujun na o-tenki / yoi tenki ga tsuzuite imasu.
  The weather has been very unpredictable / The weather has been good.

Main text

Then use one of these phrases to signal the start of the main text of the letter:

- さて、
  Sate,
  Well,

- 早速ですが、
  Sassoku desu ga,
  To get to the point,

- 実はお願いがありますが、
  Jitsu wa o-negai ga arimasu ga.
  Actually I have a request to make,

Closing Phrases

Phrases such as these are used to bring the card or letter to a close:

- くれぐれもお体をお大切に。
  Kuregure-mo o-karada o o-taisetsu ni.
  Please take good care of yourself.

- まずはお礼まで / お願いまで / お知らせまで。
  Mazu wa o-rei made/o-negai made/o-shirase made.
  Just to express thanks/to ask a favor/to let you know.

- お元気で。
  O-genki de.
  Take care.

- 皆様 / お父様 / 恵子さんによろしく。
  Mina-sama/Otōsama/Keiko-san ni yoroshiku.
  Please give my regards to everyone/your father/Keiko.

- 乱筆乱文お許しください。
  Ranpitsu ranbun o-yurushi kudasai.
  Forgive my terrible handwriting and poor grammar.

15.11   Thank you Letters

Sometimes only a letter will do. James writes to thank his professor for helping him with his research.

This letter illustrates some of the finer points of letter-writing. Note that the word 私は "I" is written at the bottom of a line, while the word

先生 "teacher" is written at the top of a line. It is also the custom to use at least two sheets of paper so the postscript and date have been taken on to a second page.

前略
皆様お変わりなくお過ごしのことと存じます。私は昨日無事に中国に帰って参りました。二年ぶりに国に帰ってちょっと戸惑いを感じています。

さて、日本滞在中は、お忙しいにもかかわらず、お世話いただき、ありがとうございました。厚く御礼申し上げます。特に先生のご親切などご指導は忘れられません。わずかな時間で充実した研究ができました。いろいろとありがとうございました。上海へいらっしゃることがありましたら、是非ご連絡ください。どうか、皆様お元気でお過ごしください

早々

山田　明　先生

林　文宝

追伸　連絡先はしばらく実家となります。

平成〇〇年四月十日

Zenryaku

Minasama o-kawari-naku o-sugoshi no koto to zonjimasu. Watashi wa sakujitsu, buji ni Chūgoku ni kaette mairimashita. Ninen-buri ni kuni ni kaette chotto tomadoi o kanjite imasu.

Sate, Nihon taizai-chū wa, o-isogashii ni mo kakawarazu o-sewa itadaki arigatō gozaimashita. Atsuku on-rei mōshi-agemasu. Toku ni, Sensei no go-shinsetsu na go-shidō wa wasureraremasen. Wazuka na jikan de jūjitsu shita kenkyū ga dekimashita. Iro-iro to arigatō gozaimashita.

Shanhai e irassharu koto ga arimashitara, zehi go-renraku kudasai.

Dōka, mina-sama o-genki de o-sugoshi kudasai.

Sōsō

Heisei○○nen shigatsu tōka

Rin Bun Ho

Yamada Akira sensei

Tsuishin: Renrakusaki wa shibaraku jikka to narimasu.

Preliminaries omitted,
I hope you are all well. The other day, I returned safely to China.
It feels a little strange to be back in my native place after being away for two years.
Thank you very much, especially considering that you were so busy, for all your help during my stay in Japan. I will never forget your kind guidance. Indeed, I was able to do some very thorough research in only a short time. Thank you for everything.
If you come to Shanghai, please be sure to let me know. I hope all of you stay in good health.
In haste.
10th April ○○th year of Heisei
Lin Wenbao
Yamada Akira sensei
P.S. My contact address for the time being will be my parents' home.

Letter to a Friend

Emily, back in the States, writes to an older woman who used to be her neighbor.

東京は寒い日が続いていることでしょう。いかがお過ごしですか。お返事を書こうと思いながら、つい書きそびれてしまいました。お許しください。

私たちは皆元気です。マイケルは仕事を変え、今、自営業のコンサルです。出張が多くなり、人と会う機会が増えたことも楽しいようです。九月にジョンが肺炎で一ヶ月近く入院しました。今はもうすっかりよくなり、学校生活を楽しんでいます。母は八十歳の誕生日を迎えましたが、元気です。よろしくとの事です。私は最近写真に興味を持ちはじめています。

どうぞ、お体にお気をつけて、お健やかにお過ごしください。

お時間がありましたら、お便りください。さようなら

平成〇〇年十二月三日

テーラー　エミリ

林　千鶴子様

Tōkyō wa samui hi ga tsuzuite iru koto deshō. Ikaga o-sugoshi desu ka?

O-henji o kakō to omoinagara, tsui kaki-sobirete shimaimashita. O-yurushi kudasai.

Watashitachi wa mina genki desu. Maikeru wa shigoto o kae, ima, jieigyō no konsaru desu. Shutchō ga ōku nari hito to au kikai ga fueta koto mo tanoshii yō desu.

Kugatsu ni Jon ga haien de, ikkagetsu chikaku nyūin shimashita. Ima wa mō sukkari yoku nari, gakkō seikatsu o tanoshinde imasu.

Haha wa hachijussai no tanjōbi o mukaemasita ga, genki desu. Yoroshiku to no koto desu. Watashi wa saikin shashin ni kyōmi o mochihajimete imasu.

Dōzo, o-karada ni o-ki o tsukete, o-sukoyaka ni o-sugoshi kudasai. O-jikan ga arimashitara, o-tayori kudasai.

Sayōnara

Heisei○○nen jūnigatsu mikka

Tērā Emiri

Hayashi Chizuko

It must be cold in Tokyo now. How are you?

I've been meaning to write back to you, but I just never got around to it. I'm very sorry.

We are all well. Michael has changed his job and is now a self employed consultant. He's often away on business and gets the chance to meet many people which he seems to enjoy.

In September, John got pneumonia and was in the hospital for nearly a month. He's completely recovered and is now enjoying school life.

My mother has had her 80th birthday but she is well. She sends her regards. As for myself, I've recently become interested in photography.

Please take care of yourself and keep well. If you have time, do write.

Goodbye

Emily Taylor

Hayashi Chizuko

15.13 Addressing Envelopes

The standard size for envelopes in Japan is 20.5 cm by 9 cm. The sender's name and address are written on the back of the envelope.

Front of envelope

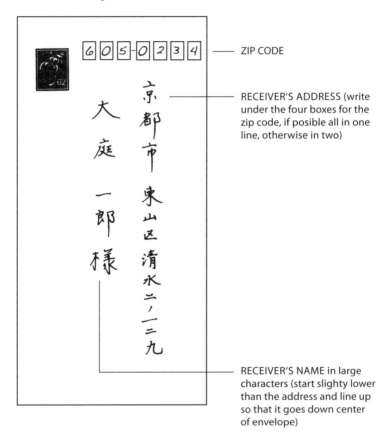

605-0234 — ZIP CODE

RECEIVER'S ADDRESS (write under the four boxes for the zip code, if possible all in one line, otherwise in two)

RECEIVER'S NAME in large characters (start slightly lower than the address and line up so that it goes down center of envelope)

Kyōto-shi, Higashiyama-ku, Kiyomizu 2-129
Ōba Ichirō-sama

Back of envelope

CROSS (write over the seal; the cross is associated with the word *shimeru*, which means "to close")

四月十日

DATE

東京都港区麻布台一〇一ー三〇三

ミッチェル　ロバート

SENDER'S NAME AND ADDRESS in small characters

1 0 6 - 0 2 3 4

ZIP CODE

Shigatsu tōka
Tōkyō-to, Minato-ku, Azabu-dai 1-10-1-303
Mitcheru Robāto

Front of envelope

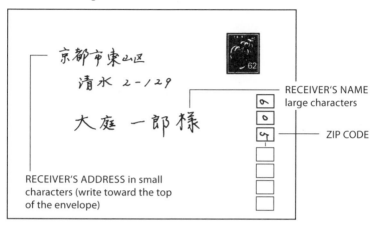

RECEIVER'S NAME
large characters

ZIP CODE

RECEIVER'S ADDRESS in small characters (write toward the top of the envelope)

Kyoto-shi, Higashiyama-ku, Kiyomizu 2 – 129
Ōba Ichirō-sama

Back of envelope

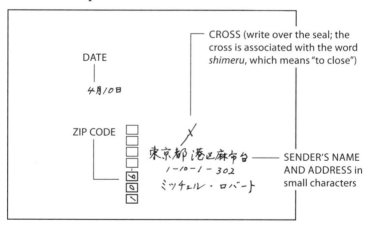

CROSS (write over the seal; the cross is associated with the word *shimeru*, which means "to close")

DATE

ZIP CODE

SENDER'S NAME AND ADDRESS in small characters

Shigatsu tōka
Tōkyō-to, Minato-ku, Azabu-dai 1-10-1-303
Mitcheru Robāto

Words and Expressions

E-MAIL

sōshin	送信	*send, send button*
tenpu (suru)	添付 (する)	*attachment, to attach*
sōfu suru	送付する	*to send*
haritsuke	貼り付け	*paste*

LETTERS

tegami	手紙	*letter*
tayori	便り	*news, letter*
hagaki	はがき	*postcard*
kansei hagaki	官製はがき	*prestamped postcard*
fūtō	封筒	*envelope*
nengajō	年賀状	*New Year cards*
tōkan suru/posuto ni ireru	投函する・ポストに入れる	*to mail a letter*
henji	返事	*reply*
shūji	習字	*handwriting*
shodō	書道	*calligraphy*

Appendix:
Respect Language –
Table of Japanese Verbs

sonkeigo, kenjōgo, teineigo
尊敬語・謙譲語・丁寧語
respectful, humble and polite language

The following table provides a guide to the different levels of politeness for some common Japanese verbs. The plain form is used for informal speech between friends and family, the –**masu** form is used in general conversation outside this circle, the honorific form is used to refer politely to others, and the humble form for referring deferentially to yourself. It covers basic usage when addressing a second person. The language for showing respect to a third person is not covered.

The passive is included in this table along with the other honorific forms as it is widely used to show respect to the person you're speaking to. However, it is not strictly an honorific, belonging rather to the group of words known as polite language. This perhaps accounts for its popularity as it may appear more informal, showing respect without putting the person on a pedestal. But take care not to overdo it.

ENGLISH	PLAIN FORM	-MASU FORM	HONORIFIC FORM	HUMBLE FORM
REGULAR VERBS (~u)				
to write	書く **kaku**	書きます **kakimasu**	お書きになります **o-kaki ni narimasu**	お書きします/ いたします **o-kaki shimasu/ itashimasu**
REGULAR VERBS (~ru)				
to send	送る **okuru**	送ります **okurimasu**	お送りになる **o-okuri ni naru**	お送りします/ いたします **o-okuri shimasu/ itashimasu**
IRREGULAR VERBS				
to do	する **suru**	します **shimasu**	なさいます **nasaimasu** されます **saremasu**	致します **itashimasu**
to be	いる **iru**	います **imasu**	いらっしゃいます **irasshaimasu**	おります **orimasu**
to exist	ある **aru**	あります **arimasu**	—	ございます **gozaimasu**
to be	である **de aru**	です **desu**	でいらっしゃいます **de irasshaimasu**	でございます **de gozaimasu**
to come	来る **kuru**	来ます **kimasu**	いらっしゃいます **irasshaimasu** おいでになります **oide ni narimasu** お見えになります **o-mie ni narimasu** 来られます **koraremasu**	参ります **mairimasu** 伺います **ukagaimasu** 上がります **agarimasu**

ENGLISH	PLAIN FORM	-MASU FORM	HONORIFIC FORM	HUMBLE FORM
to go	行く iku	行きます ikimasu	いらっしゃいます irasshaimasu おいでになります oide ni narimasu 行かれます ikaremasu	参ります mairimasu 伺います ukagaimasu
to say	言う iu	言います iimasu	おっしゃいます osshaimasu	申します mōshimasu 申し上げます shiagemasu
to think	思う omou	思います omoimasu	お思いになります o-omoi ni nari-masu 思われます omowaremasu	存じます zonjimasu
to consider	考える kangaeru	考えます kangaemasu	お考えになります o-kangae ni narimasu 考えられます kangaeraremasu	考えさせていただきます kangaesasete itadakimasu
to ask	聞く kiku	聞きます kikimasu	お聞きになります o-kiki ni narimasu 聞かれます kikaremasu	伺います ukagaimasu お聞きします o-kiki shimasu
to see	見る miru	見ます mimasu	ご覧になります goran ni narimasu 見られます miraremasu	拝見します haiken shi-masu 見せていただきます misete itadaki-masu
to visit	訪ねる tazuneru	訪ねます tazunemasu	お訪ねになります o-tazune ni nari-masu 訪ねられます tazuneraremasu	伺います ukagaimasu

ENGLISH	PLAIN FORM	-MASU FORM	HONORIFIC FORM	HUMBLE FORM
to know	知る **shiru**	知ります・ 知っています **shirimasu/ shitte imasu**	ご存知です **go-zonji desu**	存じます **zonjimasu**
to eat	食べる **taberu**	食べます **tabemasu**	召し上がります **meshiagarimasu** 食べられます **taberaremasu**	いただきます **itadakimasu**
to read	読む **yomu**	読みます **yomimasu**	お読みになります **o-yomi ni nari- masu** 読まれます **yomaremasu**	読ませていただ きます **yomasete itadakimasu**
to give	上げる※ **ageru**	上げます **agemasu**	—	差し上げます **sashiagemasu**
to give	くれる **kureru**	くれます **kuremasu**	下さいます **kudasaimasu**	—
to receive	もらう **morau**	もらいます **moraimasu**	—	いただきます **itadakimasu**

※ To give food to an animal you would use やる **yaru**.

KINSHIP TERMS

When speaking to your own or your spouse's father or mother, use **otōsan** and **okāsan**; but when speaking about them to people outside your family, use **chichi** and **haha**, respectively. Only children use **otōsan** and **okāsan** when talking about their own parents.

Usage is not so strict concerning the terms for grandparents. The terms **ojiisan** (grandfather) and **obāsan** (grandmother) can be used when speaking to friends, but otherwise the more formal terms **sofu** and **sobo** should be used.

ENGLISH	TALKING ABOUT YOUR RELATIVES		ADDRESSING YOUR RELATIVES OR TALKING ABOUT THEIR RELATIVES	
mother	母	haha	お母さん お母様	okāsan okāsama
father	父	chichi	お父さん お父様	otōsan otōsama
parents	両親	ryōshin	ご両親	go-ryōshin
elder brother	兄	ani	お兄さん お兄様	oniisan oniisama
elder sister	姉	anē	お姉さん お姉さま	onēsan onēsama
younger brother	弟	otōto	弟さん 弟様	otōtosan otōtosama
younger sister	妹	imōto	妹さん 妹様	imōtosan imōtosama
grandmother	内のおばあち ゃん 祖母	uchi no obāchan sobo	おばあさん おばあ様	obāsan obāsama
grandfather	内のおじいち ゃん 祖父	uchi no ojiichan sofu	おじいさん おじい様	ojiisan ojiisama
wife	家内 妻	kanai tsuma	奥さん 奥様	okusan okusama
husband	夫 主人	otto shujin	ご主人	go-shujin
son	息子	musuko	息子さん	musuko-san
daughter	娘	musume	お嬢さん	ojōsan
children	子供	kodomo	子供さん お子さん お子様	kodomo-san okosan okosama
uncle	叔父	oji	叔父さん 叔父様	ojisan ojisama
aunt	叔母	oba	叔母さん 叔母様	obasan obasama

JAPANESE ERA NAMES AND WESTERN CALENDAR

Era Name	Western Calendar	Era Name	Western Calendar	Era Name	Western Calendar
Meiji 43	1910	Showa 20	1945	Showa 55	1980
44	1911	21	1946	56	1981
Meiji 45 Showa 1	1912	22	1947	57	1982
2	1913	23	1948	58	1983
3	1914	24	1949	59	1984
4	1915	25	1950	60	1985
5	1916	26	1951	61	1986
6	1917	27	1952	62	1987
7	1918	28	1953	63	1988
8	1919	29	1954	Heisei 1	1989
9	1920	30	1955	2	1990
10	1921	31	1956	3	1991
11	1922	32	1957	4	1992
12	1923	33	1958	5	1993
13	1924	34	1959	6	1994
14	1925	35	1960	7	1995
Taisho 15 Showa 1	1926	36	1961	8	1996
2	1927	37	1962	9	1997
3	1928	38	1963	10	1998
4	1929	39	1964	11	1999
5	1930	40	1965	12	2000
6	1931	41	1966	13	2001
7	1932	42	1967	14	2002
8	1933	43	1968	15	2003
9	1934	44	1969	16	2004
10	1935	45	1970	17	2005
11	1936	46	1971	18	2006
12	1937	47	1972	19	2007
13	1938	48	1973	20	2008
14	1939	49	1974	21	2009
15	1940	50	1975	22	2010
16	1941	51	1976	23	2011
17	1942	52	1977	24	2012
18	1943	53	1978	25	2013
19	1944	54	1979	26	2014